Life on the Wrong Planet

H. G. Nowak
(The Barefoot Man)

DEDICATION

This book is dedicated to my white dog named "Cat" and my black dog named "Dog". If most humans were as loyal, appreciative, non-racial and friendly as these two mutts I'd have no gripe about being placed on the wrong planet.

CONTENTS

I'm not going to break it down in chapters,
but the contents of this book are about stupid
people,stupid gadgets, stupid rules and stupid laws.

The contents of this book will piss off stupid people
and that is my objective.

ACKNOWLEDGMENTS

I want to thank all idiots, numbskulls, hypocritical vicars and corrupt politicians and, of course, the Internet along with Wikipedia for making this manuscript possible. And John and Clair Upperton, two Earthlings who have patiently listened to my philosophy in shock and disbelief... yet we are still friends. They wouldn't make it on my planet.

I also want to thank Tammie Chisholm and Jenny Gabruch for their editing help – believe me I need the help. And, of course, my lovely wife Regina. I am so glad she is a misplaced Coherent like me or I would have never found her. When it comes to assessing idiots, she and I are two peas in a pod. Can't forget my friend and author Guy Harrison out in California. Next to Bill Cosby, he is the closest thing to a Coherent that I know. Check out his books at www.guypharrison.com.

When I leave my coastal hiding spot I am quickly encircled with fools; they are everywhere. However, I try to make the best of it. I am very appreciative of everything else – the sea, sun, family and health (health for the moment, that is). My mother taught me appreciation. She would respond to my moaning with the most interesting retorts.

"Mom, I don't feel good, I have a headache."

"Oh stop your whining," she would say. "Some people don't have a head."

"Mom, I need some new shoes. I have nothing but holes in this old pair."

"Oh for goodness sake, hush up, some people don't have shoes."

"Mom, I twisted my ankle playing football."

"Oh shut up, some people don't have feet."

"Mom, I hate our neighbors, they're disgusting people."

"Deal with them. You could be stuck on another planet."

And that's the brash outlook on life I was brought up with. And I'm thankful for it. I appreciate everything... except idiots.

The cover art is by the legendary Michael P. Maness. His artistic work is out of this world, so he is obviously from my planet.

Michael is an eclectic mid-south artist who sees ART in everything, everywhere. His vision evokes his peculiar view of the world: bright, colorful, interesting, with a dash of hope.

Since the age of eight, Mike has been drawing, painting, designing or writing for somebody. Spanning from limited edition posters to album covers to movie posters, for over 30 years he has been in the business of art, advertising and marketing. Michael has contributed stories and illustrations to regional and national magazines and has also worked for many Fortune 500 companies.

In 1997, Michael was diagnosed with lymphoma and bone marrow cancer. A bone marrow transplant not only got his health back on track, his brush with death gave him a new attitude and perspective on life and a new vigor that took over the direction of his craft. His unique style and iridescent colors are indicative of a new passion for life and a unique interpretation of his surroundings.

"I see the world from a different angle than most people," says Maness. "Instead of a constantly changing world, a crowd doing the expected, I paint the individual and focus on the individual's spirit to tell a story."

Four bouts with cancer, 10 returns of that beast and a brush with congestive heart failure later, Mike's generous donations of original paintings and prints have raised over $4 million for St. Jude Children's Research Hospital, the Red Door, Clay Walker's Band Against MS, the International Children's Heart Foundation, The Blues Foundation, The Susan G. Koman Foundation and over 150 other organizations.

Among Mike's numerous accolades and awards is the Keeping the Blues Alive award from the International Blues Foundation; Best of the Best in his home county in Mississippi; and the Memphis Hero award from the Orpheum Theater in Memphis, Tennessee.

His paintings can be found all over the globe, as well as seven museums and the Rock and Roll Hall of Fame in Cleveland, Ohio.

Mike's work can viewed at www.artbypm.com. Michael P. Maness is now living in Southaven, Mississippi.

Ya'll live in a perceived box,
you color within the lines,
it's a black, white, grey world,
I say open your eyes.
COLOR is an experience, a journey, a trip –
look out for bananas peels,
you might just slip.
– Michael Maness

You will find the occasional typo throughout this manuscript and there are a few good reasons for that.

1). This book has been three years in the making. It has been edited a few times, yet during editing, friends, family and the media would bring to my attention yet another humanoid blunder. I would immediately write about it and insert it into the text somewhere, forgetting, or not wanting to pay for re-editing again.

2). Often I was drinking and writing at the same time.

3). Because I'm sure no Random House or Simon and Schuster-class publisher would be brave enough to publish this book... so what does the occasional typo matter?

4). Because I can.

"Believe nothing, no matter what you read unless it agrees with your own reason and your own common sense."
– A Buddha quote

INTRODUCTION

"Common sense is NOT a gift, it's punishment. Because you have to deal with everyone who doesn't have it."

Somewhere out there in the far galaxies, through the black hole and more than three million light-years away is Planet Coherent. Coherent is an identical twin of Planet Earth. For some reason when Earth and Coherent were born, they were separated. No one knows why or when this all happened except that it happened billions of years ago. Coherent has an Africa, America, Europe, North Pole, Atlantic Ocean, Pacific Ocean and Mount Everest. There are humans, animals and plants – all identical in features to those on Earth. There are blacks, whites, Orientals and Asians. Any professor of astronomy will argue with my hypothesis. However, too often I've been asked: "What planet are you from?" This is the usual retort I get whenever I give my opinion on politics, crime and religion. Now, I'm not the least bit insulted when they question my cosmos because they are right – "I am on the wrong planet!"

Here is what I think happened. By some mistake God or a Tiki spirit or a Buddha, or whatever, made a mistake and placed me on Planet Earth. Instead, I should have gone to Earth's twin Planet Coherent. On Planet Coherent the majority of the beings are rational and logical – not all are rocket scientists or university graduates but most have basic common sense. Mixed along with the Coherents are a small percentage of dunces that belong on Planet Earth. Theses humanoids on Coherent have also been placed on the wrong planet. Now, back on Earth it's the other way around – the majority of individuals are dense dimwits who are mixed with a very small minority of sound, level-headed individuals who have been misplaced and belong on Planet Coherent. I believe that astronomers are incorrect when they say Jupiter is the largest planet in the universe. Earth must be the largest, as you need a huge planet to hold so many dummies.

So when Jah, Allah, the Almighty – or whoever – realized He put me on Earth instead of Coherent, it was too late. With all their powers, no Great Spirit could reverse the circumstance. Either they null-and-void me completely or keep me here – on Earth – with a bunch of idiots. However, to compensate me for this major setback (that I'd have to deal with all my life), the Maker (whoever he or she may be) rewarded me with a good life. During my first hour on Earth, He looked down upon me and said: "It will be OK, my son. I'll see to it that you stay reasonably healthy, happy and run-of-the-mill cute. Sorry, I can't give you handsome, gorgeous or hot – that's all been reserved for Brad Pitt who will be born 14 years from now. I'll make sure that most of your dreams come true and that you will always have a lust for pretty women, fine cigars and remote islands, where you can escape the everyday idiotic trends of this planet. This, my son, I bestow upon you for my dire mistake; my mistake of placing you on the wrong planet."

And that was it... He was gone. I started to scream in baby language, "WHAAAAAAA!" which, translated, means: "Come back here, you traitor! Don't leave me here on Planet Earth with all these fools. WHAAAAAAA!" My mother was pleased – she held a healthy boy in her arms with obvious good working vocal chords.

And so here I am. I'm not a conservative, a liberal, an atheist or Christian. I am not a democrat, a republican, an independent or socialist. I am not a racist, a bigot or a chauvinist. I am simply a lost, level-headed soul wandering around on the wrong planet. Life has been very good for me on Planet Earth; it's been a great run. I have never had to experience hard labor, I have traveled the globe, I've remained fairly healthy and most of my dreams have come true. However, as the old saying goes, "nothing is perfect", especially when you're surrounded by morons. So I'll repeat what I said just a few pages ago –"Common sense is NOT a gift, it's punishment. Because you have to deal with everyone who doesn't have it." And I might add, in my ranting and raving, I'm not only talking about Earthlings with no common sense, I am also talking about things that Earthlings manufacture that make no common sense and many of their rules, regulations and laws. Now, for the moment, let's not evaluate your common sense, and let's gauge your sense of humor. If you can't take a joke or are thin-skinned, a bigot or an overboard religious fanatic — stop reading NOW!

Here we go...

THE STUPID GAUGE

So for you, the reader, who has read this far, I will give you more of a preview of coming attractions with my "Stupid Gauge". My gauge is an imaginary instrument used to measure "Ignorancepheric" pressure. Here are some of the more celebrated examples of what's ahead and another chance to... stop reading NOW!

You can choose what should be high or low on the scale.

Francesco Schettino, the captain of the luxury cruiser Costa Concordia, claims he tripped and fell safely into a lifeboat as his ship was sinking – with 4,000 passengers aboard.

Zimbabwe President Robert Mugabe declared that he will not put a ban on ivory because elephants took up a lot of space and drank a lot of water. Elephants would have to pay for their room and board with their ivory.

Albuquerque, New Mexico court allows Stella Liebeck to sue McDonald's after she clumsily spills hot coffee on herself.

Sports hero Michael Vick invests some of his fortune in dog fighting – his stupidity cost him millions in endorsements and legal fees.

Brainless jury members for the O.J. Simpson murder trial.

Cayman Islands Prison: To seize an illicit cell phone from a teen girl, it took nine members of a Special Emergency Response Team (similar to SWAT) to retrieve the phone that was openly visible lying on her bed. The unnecessary use of force was actually retaliation. The teen, along with several other inmates, had written a complaint letter about the guards just 24 hours earlier. The teen was cuffed, bruised and her clothing torn. She required a hospital visit the following day. Later, the prison director was asked to retire early. Usually in such a case this would mean he had no choice – you retire or we fire.

Ohio school teacher Maria Waltherr-Willard claims discrimination due to her fear of children. The case is scheduled to go to court in early 2014.

Did my stupidity gauge offend you? Anger you in any way? How do you think I feel? I wouldn't have to manage my anger if people could learn to manage their stupidity. If at this point you are offended by my writings, then again, I remind you one last time – stop reading NOW! Pass this book along to someone with a sense of humor; one who is level-headed, sensible and coherent. Did I just say that you aren't level-headed, sensible or coherent? My ranting and raving, along with my bizarre, insulting, positive attitude, may not solve all the world's problems, but it will annoy enough of you to make it worth the effort.

I'M NOT THE ONLY ONE

If you are an average humanoid that belongs on Planet Earth rather than Coherent, then somewhere along the way while reading this book you will be disgusted, pissed off and will shout out obscenities towards me.

"Who does he think he is?"

"What an arrogant SOB!"

That's OK. I understand. I ask you, however, to please consider the words of others more famous and intelligent than you and I:

"Two things are infinite: the universe and human stupidity; and I'm not sure about the universe."
– Albert Einstein

"I'll take crazy over stupid any day."
– Joss Whedon

"Never underestimate the power of stupid people in large groups."
– George Carlin

"You are not entitled to your opinion. You are entitled to your informed opinion. No one is entitled to be ignorant."
– Harlan Ellison

"In politics, stupidity is not a handicap."
– Napoleon Bonaparte

"You have attributed conditions to villainy that simply result from stupidity."
– Robert A. Heinlein, The Green Hills of Earth

"Evil isn't the real threat to the world. Stupid is just as destructive as evil, maybe more so, and it's a hell of a lot more common. What we really need is a crusade against stupid. That might actually make a difference."
– Jim Butcher, Vignette

"The two most common elements in the universe are hydrogen and stupidity."
– Harlan Ellison

"He had just about enough intelligence to open his mouth when he wanted to eat, but certainly no more."
– P.G. Wodehouse

"Mary wished to say something very sensible, but knew not how."
– Jane Austen, Pride and Prejudice

"Stupidity is the same as evil if you judge by the results."
– Margaret Atwood, Surfacing

"There is more stupidity than hydrogen in the universe, and it has a longer shelf life."
– Frank Zappa

"Talk sense to a fool and he calls you foolish."
– Euripides, Bacchae

"I've always believed that a person is smart. It's people that are stupid."
– Marilyn Manson, The Long Hard Road Out of Hell

"If your brains were dynamite there wouldn't be enough to blow your hat off."
– Kurt Vonnegut, Timequake

"In the universe it may be that] primitive life is very common and intelligent life is fairly rare. Some would say it has yet to occur on Earth."
– Stephen Hawking

"He was stupid. If I killed everyone who was stupid, I wouldn't have time to sleep."
– Tamora Pierce

"Intelligence minus purpose equals stupidity."
– Toba Beta, Master of Stupidity

"I have defined the hundred percent American as ninety-nine percent an idiot."
– George Bernard Shaw

"Life is tough but it's tougher when you're stupid."
– John Wayne

"The earth is a great piece of stupidity."
– Victor Hugo, Les Misérables

"Our lives are businesses that are sometimes run by idiots."
– Patrick Reinken, Omicron

"I'd rather be dumb in hell, than to be stupid in heaven."
– ?

ELUCIDATION

Earth – The third planet from the Sun, having a sidereal time period of revolution around the Sun of 365.26 days. Population estimated to be around 7.118 billion. Most of those are Earthlings. Approximately 2,289 are misplaced Coherents.

Coherent – Twin to Earth (separated at birth) approximately three million light-years from Earth. Population estimated to be around 7.118 billion. Most of those are Coherents. Approximately 2,289 are misplaced Earthlings.

"You're on the wrong planet!" When this assertion is targeted at me, this is a correct statement.

"He/she's on the right planet." This is when I am making reference to an Earthling who belongs on Earth rather than Coherent.

Stuporous – Another planet where Earthlings from Coherent are banished for crimes against common sense.

TAKE NOTE

The "out-of-this-planet" views and opinions of the author are not necessarily the views and opinions of the editors, the printers and majority of the Earthlings that survive on Planet Earth. The author is not responsible for the actions of any Earthlings after they have read this book.

COMMON SENSE – WHAT IS IT?

Well let's start with this book. Let's say you needed a book on astronomy for a very important project. Let's say you are very intelligent. Let's say you noticed the word "planet" on the cover of this book and then you read the entire introduction in the opening pages as you wait in line to pay for this book at a Barnes & Noble. When you reach the cashier, you buy this book with your last $15 until payday. Then, when you get home you are perturbed and feel cheated because there was no scientific information in this book about Mars, Pluto or Saturn. Well, then, you have no common sense and you are on the right planet – EARTH. Any rational-thinking person would have realized right from the first sentence that this is not a book about the planets. Sorry – NO REFUNDS for idiots.

I consider myself a very happy, stress-free individual – most of the time. Yet, there are things on Planet Earth that truly vex me; one of them is stupidity. This book is my way of screaming at the top of the highest summit: "HELP, I'M ON THE WRONG PLANET!"

I'll give you another example: Have you ever (from a man's point of view) seen a young, very beautiful girl with a cigarette dangling from the side of her mouth, orange neon-spiked hair and every inch of her body covered with tattoos, not to mention pierced lips, nipples, eyebrows, tongue, nose and who knows what else? Don't you just wanna go up to her and whack her across the head? I do. Now if such a sight doesn't bother you, if you don't cringe or roll your eyes... you definitely are on your planet and you don't belong on my planet – Coherent. Get ready: you will see the word **"Whack"** often in this book. Planet Earth is full of dimwits. You see them every day and that's why I hate going into town. On Grand Cayman, where I make my home, I see my share of stupidity. Not that stupidity is limited to Cayman. It's common almost any place on Earth. It's just that on a small island the stupidity is more condensed and noticeable.

Some examples:

A taxi driver in a mini-bus stops at a blind curb right smack in the middle of his lane to pick up passengers when there is an entire acre of land to pull into.

Some daft rapper spins his wheels (in the middle of downtown) burning off 50 percent of the tire just to show you how fast he can travel 20 yards.

In the 100-degree, stifling tropical heat, some clown is wearing a woolen-hood parka and sunglasses in an attempt to look cool.

A politician who makes US$120,000 per year (tax free) is requesting an increase in salary.

Give me a break. My dogs have more common sense; they want nothing except food and water and, in the scorching heat, they take a swim in the sea or nap in the shade. On the Planet Coherent (where I belong) daftly beings would be picked up and converted into human cannonballs and shot into outer space to Planet Stuporous. Man, do I hate going to town... I'm on the wrong planet.

Logic is scarce on Planet Earth.

"Never cut what you can untie."
– Joseph Joubert

On my planet, Coherent, there are some individuals roaming around who are pissed off because they, like myself, have been put on the wrong planet. They have their complaints about Coherent, as I have my complaints about Earth. These are Earthlings on the wrong planet. For example, on Coherent a child molester is castrated and his photo is placed on the front page of the Rational Enquirer (Coherent's version of that popular Earth tabloid). Now, the misplaced Earthlings on Planet Coherent are distressed because they would like to openly protest the castration of anyone; they consider it inhumane. But they know better; because on my planet anyone who has sympathy for a neutered child molester is exiled to Planet Stuporous. Being sent to Stuporous is much like being banished to Guantanamo Bay or Auschwitz.

I am conscious that I'm on the wrong planet when I read the case of a 16-year-old boy who had an affair with his seductive 31-year-old schoolteacher, Miss Amber Jennings. She would even send him naked pictures of herself via email. Then what happens? They arrest the teacher for making the kid the happiest boy on Planet Earth. Makes no sense to me. On my planet, that teacher would get a medal or a raise in salary. When you are a young man in puberty it's absolutely NORMAL to want to get laid by a woman... an older woman (not a grandma). Any 16-year-old boy who doesn't have such a fantasy is simply gay. When I was 16, I had many damp dreams about some of my schoolteachers. I would often drop my pencil just to get a peek up my history teacher's skirt. Had she ever molested me that would have been pure ecstasy – a dream come true. I would have been the envy of the football team. My father would have been jealous and my mother would have asked the teacher to wash the sheets before she left my room.

One Earthling distinction that's common on Coherent is slimy lawyers. Except on Coherent, things work in reverse. In other words, our defense lawyers are not allowed to lie for their client. They can, however, lie for the victim. Just imagine it:

Defense Lawyer – "Your Honor, my client says that he only kicked this poor little girl's dog. The evidence, however, will show sir – he ran over her dog."

"Intentionally?" asks the judge.

The lawyer whispers to his heartless animal-hater client: "Did you run over the dog intentionally?"

"I didn't run over her damn dog... I only kicked it," the defendant responds.

"Yes, your Honor, intentionally."

"OK... hang him!"

Now take the same circumstance on Planet Earth:

Defense lawyer – "Your Honor, my client did not run over this little girl's dog, he only kicked it. He saw a tick on the dog so he was attempting to boot the tick off the dog."

"Then why do I have a photo here of a squashed dog on the highway showing this same little girl who is sitting in this courtroom crying next to her dead dog and your client's car in the background with his license plate number clearly visible?" asks the judge.

"Well, sir, what I think happened is that this clever little girl, who is very computer savvy, fabricated this photo with the help of Photoshop."

"Did you do that?" the judge asks, looking at the little girl.

"I don't have a computer. I want my doggie back."

The bemused judge says, "Someone must be lying in this courtroom."

The defense lawyer jumps from his seat. "Sir, it must be the little girl. After all, my client is paying me a lot of money to deceive the court and get him out of this mess."

"Good point," agrees the judge. "Case dismissed, and all costs to be charged to the little girl."

I have a few lawyer friends (very few) and I've told them my fictional "little girl-doggie" story, only to make my point that lawyers twist and misconstrue and swindle the system to protect the criminal – rather than show compassion for the victim. "Hogwash," one responded. "Foolish gibberish," said the other. "That could never happen. Our judicial system is the best on this planet."

"What about the O.J. Simpson case? What's your opinion on that?" I ask. "Well that... that was very ingenious defense work by a dream team that was paid tons of money."

I was looking to get a "guilty or not guilty" response from them – instead I got money talk. You see what I mean – I'm on the wrong planet! Shakespeare said it best: "The first thing we do, let's kill all lawyers."

When you do finally get some hardened criminal behind bars on this planet they have an exercise room, color TV, three square meals per day, and some even get the use of a trailer so they can have sex with their wife, lover or partner, no matter what the gender. And should you refuse them of such luxuries they will protest, riot and burn down the prison... and here come the lawyers. Not on my planet.

I have made many attempts to locate the author of the "Jail vs. Nursing Home" for several reasons. I want to meet the source face-to-face, shake that person's hand and buy that person a few drinks and talk about Coherent. Anyone with such a clever, intellectual view must be from my planet. This person, like myself, has been displaced on Earth, a planet where common sense barely survives. If, by some coincidence, this person gets hold of my book, please don't sue me for plagiarism, for I applaud your rationale.

Let's put the senior citizens in jail. This way, the seniors would have access to showers, hobbies and walks. They'd receive unlimited free prescriptions, dental and medical treatment, and they'd receive money instead of paying it out. They would have constant video monitoring, so they could be helped instantly if they fell, or needed assistance. Bedding would be washed twice a week, and all clothing would be ironed and returned to them. A guard would check on them every 20 minutes and bring their meals and snacks to their cell. They would have access to a library, weight room, spiritual counseling, pool, education, simple clothing, shoes, slippers, pajamas, and legal aid would be free on request. They would also have private, secure rooms with an outdoor exercise yard and gardens. Each senior could have a PC, TV, radio and daily phone calls. There would be a board of directors to hear complaints, and the guards and nurses would have a code of conduct that would be strictly adhered to. Now, as for the "criminals" they would be placed in a nursing home. Here, they would get cold food, and be left all alone and unsupervised. Lights off at 8 p.m., and showers once a week. They would live in a tiny room, pay $5,000 per month and have no hope of ever getting out... justice for all.

On Coherent, a hardened criminal gets water and a loaf of bread each day. If you complain, we take away the water... so shut up. I guarantee you on my planet there are no overcrowded prisons. The state would not pick up the expense for an army of security guards because no one would ever consider escaping – that's unheard of on planet Coherent as we'd simply send a posse of redneck National Rifle Association members after you. Bows and arrows would also be allowed, and the reward for an escapee would be most enticing. And, how about those people who stand outside a prison on execution day with a Bible in one hand and a candle in the other? They piss me off. Here some guy shot up kids, grandma and burger-turners at some McDonald's – the culprit was on the security video – and he has been found guilty. He's appealed five times and the state has spent millions on his defense and the governor has turned down his request for a pardon. Still, however, a crowd of ignorant, anti-capital punishment liberals are crying and wailing outside the prison gates. No matter how I try to justify their stupidity, I simply don't get it. And WHY spend millions of the public purse on a criminal when you have the guy on the video camera committing the crime? Just delete him from the planet; it will make traffic move faster. I am on the wrong planet!

I should never watch the TV show "Cops". It's a great show, it's addictive... but man do I get in a rage after a two-hour marathon of "Cops" – and a six-pack of beer. Now that's a show with some real proof of what I'm talking about – idiots infiltrate this planet. I watch in anger as teenage punks in a stolen car speed through residential areas ignoring stop signs, pedestrians and common sense. They flip the vehicle, slam into a telephone pole... and walk out. They LIVE! Damn, that pisses me off. If that isn't enough, the cops can't kick them or shoot them. If they do, the cops get fired... go figure. And if that's not enough, two hours later the punks are out on bail snickering about their high speed disregard...? Where is Robo Cop? Where is Charles Bronson? Where is Clint Eastwood? One of my favorite movies of all time is the original "Death Wish". The Charles Bronson character and, of course, Harry Callahan are from my planet.

"I know what you're thinking. Did he fire six shots or only five? Well, to tell you the truth, in all this excitement, I've kind of lost track myself. But being as this is a 44 Magnum, the most powerful handgun in the world, and would blow your head clear off, you've got to ask yourself one question: Do I feel lucky? Well, do ya punk?"
– Harry Callahan (Dirty Harry)

"Most people would die sooner than think; in fact, they do."
– Bertrand Russell

THE CHURCH

I'm seated with a band mate on a charter flight from Charlotte to Miami when the subject of religion comes up. We debate an issue that never has a satisfactory resolve, yet somehow it always comes up. Because of its complexity and hypocrisy, it's one of my favorite subjects. As I'm about to get very passionate expressing my point of view on God, evolution and hell, my friend says, "Be careful what you say – we are 20,000 feet in the air." I giggle at his quip and respond, "Oh, relax. If it's your time to go, it's your time to go." "I'm not worried about my time to go," he says. "I'm worried if it's the pilot's time to go." See what I mean? Discussing religion usually ends up in a "cul-de-sac". Religion, Christianity, the church, faith... I shouldn't go there, because when I do I always get in trouble – but I can't help myself. I need to tell you about religion on Planet Coherent. There is none!

No, it's not a planet of atheists; it's just that most Coherents don't believe you have to go to church to go to heaven – because we don't believe in heaven. Well, let me take that back... on my planet, heaven is a good cigar, good sex, fine wine, fishing... anything like that; whatever makes you happy. For example, castrating child molesters can be considered a heavenly act on my planet. Actually, living on Coherent instead of Earth is heaven... wish I was there. What an Earthly mess when you think about it: Muslims hate the Jews, Protestants hate the Catholics, Hindus hate Christians, and I hate Seventh-day Adventists knocking at my door looking for a hand-out... that pisses me off!

I have no reservations in saying that I hate the likes of Benny Hinn, Jimmy Swaggart and Jim Bakker. These slime buckets are reverse Robin Hoods: they take from the poor and give to the rich – the rich being themselves. As you can already tell, the dilemma of being placed on the wrong planet has me livid about many issues, but none anger me more that televangelists. Benny Hinn's ministries have at one time taken in about $200 million yearly, yet the self-proclaimed prophet asks his flock to give more so he can purchase a $36-million private Gulfstream jet. The congregation is awestruck at the request, yet "If brother Hinn needs it, we will provide" and the worshipers fill the collection plates. And what about the healing thing where Mr. Hinn touches the forehead of the sick and dying, and the believer falls backwards to the amazement of millions who watch on TV and the thousands that fill the stadium. As fast as you can say "Glory, Halleluiah" the saved are cancer-free, the paralyzed toss away their wheelchairs and the blind can see. Pleeeeese ...how can anyone be so stupid and believe these crooks? It has me fuming... X*@ %! Yet here on Planet Earth, many do believe. The devout zombies dig deep in their pockets to prove their religious zeal – just in case God is watching.

Why wasn't God watching when the stage caved in at a Christian rock concert in Abbotsford, British Columbia where some 40 young people were hurt, some seriously? Think about it... here are young Christians, screaming, singing, praying and jumping up and down to the glory of God when they could be selling drugs or performing other mischievous deeds. The rock band is delivering a positive message... and yet, the stage caves in. At the same time, somewhere on the other side of town some rapper is grabbing his testicles on stage, encouraging the audience to "slap the bitch" and "shoot the pigs"... and that concert goes off without a flaw.

I speak to God sometimes... "God, please let this be a huge snapper on the end of my line"... "OMG that hurts – make the pain go away"... "God I promise to go to church if you make this book a million dollar seller"... "God please see to it that the hurricane heads in a different direction." In all those incidents, He wasn't listening. On the island of Cayman Brac, Hurricane Paloma hit in 2008 and it's been told by many Brackers that every church except one was destroyed, yet every bar except one survived. Many Brackers are devout souls and I'm sure as the hurricane was moving rapidly towards them there was much praying going on – so why did God let them down? Please don't give me that old cliché line: "GOD WORKS IN MYSTERIOUS WAYS." Sorry, I'm not buying it.

What irony: Pope John Paul II, during his reign, was the most religious figure on the planet, this planet, not mine. He would drive around surrounded by 3cm of bulletproof glass. Why is that? After all, the Pope talks to God every day. He is God's representative to over a billion Catholics on Planet Earth. So why can't God stop a bullet for his chief executive officer, the Pope? Then there was Pastor Fred Williams from the First Baptist Church of Maryville, Illinois who was giving his sermon, praying, singing hymns and asking for donations when a guy walks into the church and shoots him dead. "Dead Fred" tried to hold up the Bible to defend himself, yet the godly pastor got it anyway. POW! Right between the eyes.

On March 28, 1994, the *Chicago-Sun Times* did a sad story on a tornado that hit the Goshen Methodist Church in Piedmont, Alabama killing 19 worshippers, including children in their Easter outfits. Worshippers say they heard the wind against the church – and then the lights went out. Man, that story blows me away (no pun intended). What about the 2006 shooting in the Amish community of Nickel Miles, Pennsylvania? This one really makes me want to toss a Bible. The Amish are some of the nicest, purest, bighearted people on this planet; in fact they are so compassionate they forgave the scumbag who shot five children in their one-room school house. One Amish father noted of the killer, "He had a mother and a wife and a soul and now he's standing before a just God." A just God? Is that what he said? A just God would not have let this happen. That Amish father needs a good whack across the head with his straw hat.

The above stories are gloomy, distressing and totally perplexing. Having said that, I am not giving up on God altogether. What I am saying is that before I put on my Sunday best and drop 10 percent of my salary in a collection plate, show me some proof that this good spirit (a just God) is sitting in heaven watching over me. Considering the true narratives listed above, any common sense-thinking person would be bewildered; and bewildered I am. What about the dense parishioners who are so sedated by the Bible that they have become Harry Potter protesters? They don't want their children reading about magic, wizards or playing the game of quidditch on a flying broomstick. Don't they get it? The children are reading instead of hanging out on the street corner. I've never read a Harry Potter hardback from start to end, though my children have read them all. I do know the thick manuscripts contain no vulgar or sexual writings, no crude four-letter words, and no illustrations of naked witches (if they had, I might have read a few copies). Also, the Potter books contain no magic potion recipes that could be used to blow up a school, so what's the issue here? Depending on which planet you're from, one could say the Bible (which outsells Harry Potter) is filled with magical stories. What about the guy walking on water and turning water into wine? Then there's his good friend Moses who parted the Red Sea at the wave of his staff (the staff could be considered a magic wand). Man, I need friends like that. Imagine it – someone separates the sea while I fill a huge pot with lobster, fish and scallops. Later, as I prepare a seafood feast, I send my other friend down to the shore (the one who can turn water into wine) and he returns with buckets of chilled chardonnay – now that's magic. I doubt that J.K. Rowling's wizard character Albus Dumbledore could come up with such miraculous feats. Some devout Christians have tagged Harry Potter books as the most evil and dangerous set of books to be released in the last century. These self-righteous hypocrites need a good whack across the head with a Moses staff. I doubt that author J. K. Rowling is paying them any mind. She's too busy depositing her millions in any bank that has vaults large enough to hold it all. Good for her and, as long as she's not giving 10 percent to the church, she's from my planet.

The South Pacific, I've been there often, sailing around dream islands with such romantic names as Tahiti, Bora-Bora, Manihiki, Samoa... I've studied the history of the islands and there was a time when these Edens were a place of free love, a place free of garments or fashion, free of disease, a place of happy savages. Then came the sailors, the whalers and then the final nail in the coffin, the missionaries with their Bibles. The Puritans destroyed their tikis and burned the grass skirts. They dressed the olive-skinned beauties in hot, uncomfortable clothing from neck to toe and banned fornication underneath the coconut trees. Here come the missionaries and there went the neighborhood. It's a sad story that has a completely different ending on my planet.

On my planet – for those who do believe in God – God does not work in mysterious ways, he works in practical ways. On Coherent, God performs godly acts. The tornado that hit the Goshen Methodist Church would have been diverted towards the state prison. Nineteen rapists, muggers or molesters in orange jumpsuits would have died instead of children in their Easter outfits. Pastor Fred Williams' Bible would have stopped the bullet and Benny Hinn's Lear jet (with him inside) would crash into the side of a mountain somewhere in a remote part of India and the heat of the jet fuel would melt Benny's gold Rolex, gold rings and gold medallions into one huge clump of shiny precious metal to be later found by some poor peasant farmer with 15 kids. A hurricane would have blown the missionaries ships off course, in the direction of the North Pole where they could meet their maker – a hungry polar bear. As sadistic and heartless as my theory may sound, you can't say that I'm not a believer. I believe my "make believe" planet is a better place than a world of Benny Hinns, missionaries and badly steered tornados.

When I lived in Hawaii, I once heard the story of a newly appointed governor to the American-claimed territories in the South Pacific. The tale goes that after the WWII defeat of Japan, the governor and his wife, a steadfast Christian, arrived by warship in Saipan. As they stepped off the plank she was appalled at the topless maidens dancing in grass skirts. She insisted that this immoral tradition must end immediately. How disgusting: smiling, pretty maidens with flowers in their hair, dancing completely topless. She pressured her husband to order thousands of army standard T-shirts, which she personally helped pass out to the islanders. The natives were very appreciative of the gift and the governor's wife was very pleased with their enthusiasm as she demonstrated the proper way to cover up succulent breasts. That following Sunday, in church, she fell to her knees – "Thank you Jesus for guiding me and giving me the wisdom to defeat and outcast Satan from these beautiful islands." After the church service the governor and his wife took a leisurely drive around the island. She was taken aback to see all the women, from teenagers to grandmothers, had cut two holes in front of the T-shirts to reveal their bouncy boobies. Oh, I love that story.

December 14, 2012, Newton, Connecticut, U.S.

A Christmas cool was in the air. Trees were already decorated for Jesus' birthday... which according to the New Testament (for those of you who do not know) Jesus is the son of God. Children were sitting on Santa's knee and visions of sugar-plums danced in their heads. And then it happened...

Dressed in black fatigues and a military vest, Adam Lanza walked into a Newton Connecticut school and opened fire. Within minutes, 26 people were dead at Sandy Hook Elementary School – 20 of them children. I'm confused, and meaning no disrespect to the Christians who live in the town of Newton, how is it that after this massacre can they go to church for a prayer vigil for the victims and poor families? I honestly don't understand. Why are they not demanding an answer from Msgr. Jerald A. Doyle, administrator of the Diocese of Bridgeport, which oversees the Newtown Catholic church? I would want to know why we have been betrayed. The Church claims God is watching us and loves us, and we are his children... then why did he let this happen 11 days before the second most religious holiday on this messed up planet. Why?

Why didn't God jam the gun? Why didn't He put a heart attack on the shooter? I'm sorry, it just doesn't add up. Why pray to Him for healing or a raise in salary or to catch a big fish if He's not listening and watching over us? Caribbean and U.S. prisons house their share of sexual child offenders. Why didn't God just get rid of 26 of them? Why not? I don't get it. My confusion does not make me an atheist; it makes me logical, rational and coherent (in my opinion). But then, I'm on the wrong planet.

News Flash Extra – December 22, 2012 – Three days before Christmas

The woman at Juniata Valley Gospel Church in Franktown Pennsylvania had cooked food the day before for the funeral of the church's longtime pastor. The church was still reeling from the Rev. David McCaulley's death when the woman returned to decorate its hall. Moments later bullets ripped through a window and she was dead. Three days before Christmas... where was GOD?

News Flash – December 24, 2012 – one day before Christmas – Christmas Eve

People around the world were celebrating the birth of Jesus. They prayed, gave tidings and prayed some more and most actually believed God was listening. At the same time a man convicted of killing his grandmother ambushed firefighters, fatally shooting two of them as they arrived to battle a blaze in upstate New York. Two other volunteer firefighters were wounded in the attack in the Rochester-area town of Webster. A police officer from the nearby town of Greece suffered minor shrapnel wounds when his vehicle was hit by gunfire. Investigators believe the suspect, William Spengler, 62, set the original fire, then likely set himself up on a beam with a clear view of the scene and started shooting. God, we know it's Jesus' birthday... but you need to go to work. You need to stop this carnage and for pragmatic agnostics as myself, you need to show some proof that you are a caring God. These killings just don't send the right message. Why did brave firefighters die from an idiot's bullet one day before Christmas? Please talk to me the next time... I have a long list of scum-bags that, in my opinion, should be assassinated.

Flashback – 1953, December 25 – Sakvice, Czechoslovakia – Christmas day

A local train was standing in Sakvice station when the Prague-Bratislava express train collided with it. One hundred and eighty-six people were killed.

Dec. 26 – Boxing Day, 2004 – one day after Christmas

An earthquake triggered a series of devastating tsunamis along the coasts of most land masses bordering the Indian Ocean, killing over 230,000 people in 14 countries, and inundating coastal communities with waves up to 30 meters (98 feet) high... And people around the world prayed. Prayed to who? A loving God? So HELP me God... I just don't get it

My son and I, along with a couple, were sitting on my porch having some cold beers and puffing on a Cuban stogie. It was an unusual gray day and thunder clouds were evident in the distance. My son asked, "How is the book coming along dad?" Well, I went into a long spiel on this chapter concerning religion. "Oh no," he said. "Dad, please don't go there." I ignored his request and discussed the Pope, Pastor Fred Williams and Benny Hinn, expressing my uncertainty and wary position on the subject. Well, from the heavens, through the dark clouds, a bolt from the blue shook the earth beneath us. The lightning strike had the dogs howling and running for cover, the phone lines were razed and we all looked at each other through saucer eyes. Though I was truly startled, I would not back down. I looked into the black clouds and said, "OK, God that was good, but I am not deleting this section from my book – just yet." Then I ran into the house where I cowered under the dining room table with my dogs. My guests made tracks and my son remarked as he drove away, "Dad, you are on the wrong planet. I am going to stay a good distance from you till you finish this chapter of your book." The storm passed as fast it materialized. Soon the sky had cleared and I was sitting alone in awe of my surroundings, appreciative of the swaying palms, the gin-clear lagoon and my now happy dogs playing on the beach. I'm not sure if some spirit put me on the wrong planet, however, I looked up towards the blue and said, "Thank you for everything."

"To you I'm an atheist – to God I'm a loyal oppositionist."
– Woody Allen

JESUS CAMP

It's sort of becoming old-fashioned, this thing called "summer camp". I remember it as a place where my parents would send us for three or four weeks during the summer so they didn't have to deal with me, my sister and two brothers. A place where you'd learn canoeing, archery and badminton. A place where you'd eat hot dogs, pork n' beans and macaroni n' cheese for most of your stay. It can be fun for some and hideous for others, meaning hideous for the camp counselors. I know. I was a camp counselor once back in the early '70s. This was a different sort of camp, located at Rum Point in the Cayman Islands. The clientele were also dissimilar to those camping in the pine forests up north. Here, you learned to scuba dive, water-ski and fish. At Rum Point Summer Camp the parents weren't in a separate state – they were in a separate country – and their kids were best described in two words: "spoiled brats". They would not settle for hot dogs and beans; they simply paid off the local handyman who would deliver fried chicken, steamed lobster and beer from the nearest restaurant. In this day and age with Internet, Xboxes and 538 channels on your 90-inch HD 3D TV, three weeks of badminton would be downright mind-numbing. My stepfather forced me to go to church, Sunday school, church picnics and summer Baptist prayer revivals. Not that he was passionate about any sort of religion; in fact, he never went to church. I was, however, the eldest of the siblings; the babysitter of my brothers and sister and the church was summer camp. Sending your children to church as often as you could during the summer months served two purposes for my stepfather: he could get rid of us and, at the same time, look good in the community.

"Now there's a good father. He's raising some fine children. They go to Sunday school seven days a week."

"Oh praise Jesus; they're going to grow up to be good Christians."

BULLSHIT! After we were old enough to rebel, not one of us has ever gone to church since, except to get married. I think we've spent more time in jail than in a pew. As you read on, remember I'm not an atheist. You could categorize me as a very skeptical agnostic.

Then there's Jesus Camp – how did I miss out on going to that? It's a place where Christianity and brainwashing merge to convert normal kids into Jesus freaks. The "Kids on Fire School of Ministry" was a Christian summer camp located just outside Devils Lake, North Dakota. What an irony; Jesus aficionados camping out by the Devils Lake. The place was run by Becky Fischer and her ministry or cult or doomsday advocates; whatever you want to call them. At the camp, Fischer stressed the need for children to purify themselves in order to be part of the "army of God". She strongly believes that children need to be in the forefront of turning America toward conservative Christian values. She also feels that Christians need to focus on training kids since "the enemy" (Islam) is focused on training theirs. Fisher also taught her students science, as in her believe that global warming is a political speculation, that the speculation stems from temperatures being higher in the summer months, that America's temperature has only risen by 0.6 °F, and therefore, the rise is not important. Other interesting lessons are urging children to join the fight to end abortion in America. Children are shown a series of plastic models of developing fetuses while they have their mouths covered with red tape that had "Life" written across it.

These holy brainwashers are in the same category as Satan himself. If there is a hell I want to go there because I am sure I will meet Fischer and her Ministry associates and give them all a good "whack" with the devil's staff. They instill bullshit on children – kids who could be fishing or reading a Penthouse magazine rather than the Watchtower. Religion is probably the most accepted of all hypocrisies proven with the likes of Becky Fischer, Benny Hinn and Jim Swaggart; they all lie in their serenity.

In 2006 Becky Fischer gladly appeared in a documentary about her summer camp. I can imagine what she was thinking – the more publicity, the more disciples and more money in the collection plate. The film "Jesus Camp" was nominated for

Best Documentary Feature at the 79th Academy Awards. Well, well. It seems the Devil, who was fishing over by his lake, had a big smile on his face. "Jesus Camp" did not win the Oscar; however it caused so much controversy that the camp closed shortly after. Why didn't Jesus come to Fischer's rescue? Your guess is as good as mine.

"The devil loves nothing better than the intolerance of reformers."
– James Russell Lowell

STUPID PEOPLE – POOR ANIMALS

They are wild, hungry and undomesticated, so let's NOT fault animals when they attack and decide to have some fool for lunch; put the blame on those stupid people who tend to get bitten! In most cases I cheer for the animals that rip someone's arm off in a zoo. "Why did you stick your hand through the gate... idiot? To what? Get a better photo?" Let's reverse the situation; what if some lions threw you in a cage where, every day of the week, you were bored out of your mind. No parties... no football... no booze, just a bunch lions and their cubs on the other side of the cage throwing stones at you. Then the opportunity for payback arises. Some hairy paw reaches in your cage to tease you. Think about it – wouldn't you attempt some revenge for your loss of freedom, maybe rip off a tail or paw? It's sad to know how many animals have been pointlessly killed, displaced and imprisoned due to man's stupidity. Some mammals are even taught to flip in the air for a sardine. Then there was Timothy Treadwell who had a fixation with man-eating grizzly bears. On Sunday, Oct. 5, 2003, Treadwell and his girlfriend Amy were killed and partially eaten by a huge grizzly. It was the first time in the

85-year history of Alaska's Katmai National Park that anyone had been killed by a bear. So why were Timothy and Amy eaten? Well, there are many opinions floating around the icy rivers of Alaska, but mine is that Timothy was stupid. Why would anyone intentionally hang out with grizzlies? And poor Amy... she didn't want to be there in the first place. Later, the poor grizzly that had just finished a breakfast of human legs and rib bone was shot by the rangers. The bear was just doing what comes natural to him – eating meat. Timothy was just doing what is natural for an Earthling – being stupid.

Fifty-year-old Jayaprakash Bezbaruah was attacked and killed by a tiger. He and his family were visiting the Gauhati Zoo in north-eastern India. When they came to the cage with Bengal tigers the man started shooting photos. Mr. Bezbaruah wanted a close-up shot, so he did what any dumb human would do; he climbed over the small fence separating the visitors from the actual cage. This followed with a second dim-witted act; he decided to put his hand and camera inside the cage in between the bars. The moment the caged tigers saw their opportunity for reprisal, they attacked. And there in front of his family Bezbaruah became lunch to some pissed off tigers... pissed off for being imprisoned without as much as a trial. His arm was ripped right off his shoulder and he died of massive loss of blood. What a moron. If he wanted a close up shot of a Bengal tiger, why not Google it. Hopefully the tigers weren't destroyed.

Then there's the sad story of a Michigan girl named Charlotte. She was only three months old when she was lying in her crib unsupervised and the family's pet raccoon crawled into her crib and mangled her face. The pet raccoon was removed from the forest and incarcerated in some suburbia household with a bunch of careless schmucks. Raccoons can carry rabies, an illness that can be lethal and is transmitted by bites. In the 10 years since she was attacked Charlotte has had five reconstructive surgeries on her face. She also needs to undergo surgery to replace her mauled ear. One can only imagine what poor Charlotte has gone through because her parents had a pet raccoon! After the mauling, Charlotte and her brother were taken from their parents, who lost custody. Finally, Social Services did something right.

Why wait till some poor child is mauled or disfigured for life before you return the wild to the wild where they belong; the raccoon should have been left in the forest. Charlotte, if you are reading this I have a suggestion. Find a sleazy lawyer and sue them, your parents, that is. The rare, hard-to-find dumb people on Coherent who insist on keeping wild animals for pets are themselves caged. After a few months of lock up and eating cat food pebbles they usually come to their senses. People seem to have a deep-seated desire to tame wild creatures, and it's not fair to the animal or the child who gets caught in the crosshairs of their parents' stupidity and ego. Then there was the pet hawk that attacked a toddler. The toddler was nearly blinded after a pet hawk ripped his face with its talons as the little guy was playing in a park. And, of course, there's the well publicized chimp attacked on Charla Nash. There's no sense in myself trying to find words to compete with the horrible images of Charla which you can see online. And when you put a 10,000 pound whale with a surname of "KILLER" into an aquarium and then enter the orca's cubicle too many times, something will eventually happen – someone will die and some have. There is no record of a Killer Whale in the wild ever killing a human.

August 6, 2013 – In the Canadian town of Campbellton, New Brunswick, two young boys sleeping at their friend's home above an exotic pet store were strangled to death by a python that escaped its caged enclosure. The snake was an African rock python between 14 and 16 feet long. The unidentified boys were 5 and 7 years old, the police said. They were believed to be brothers who were on a sleepover at the owner's apartment, according to the *National Post*. Now the question is... what in the world is an African python doing in northern Canada? Even in August I'm sure the African snake was shivering with cold, bearing in mind its true home was 7,000 miles away to the south. The snake was stuck in a cage and he was pissed – the python was on the wrong planet. "This is just one vicious animal," Kenneth Krysko, a herpetologist at the Florida Museum of Natural History in Gainesville, said in a 2009 *National Geographic* article. He said African pythons are "so mean they come out of the egg striking." It's sad that two young boys died because some Earthling needed to cage this dangerous reptile that belonged in the jungles of Africa. I thought better of "Canucks." Poor, poor animals.

The following is from well informed Coherent intellect: *"We allow them to multiply and even pay them to do so (welfare, grocery cards), why can't we help them dispose of themselves as well? The next time some fat slug wanders into a dangerous animal enclosure, let's help them out by keeping them locked in. The more of these dolts we delete from society, the better."* MAKES SENSE TO ME!

If you look up the suffix "phile" there is a longer list than one would imagine. Everything from pedophiles to necrophiles (a necrophile is someone attracted to the dead). There are even nice "philes" like myself. I'm like a halophile. I'm attracted to saltwater. Places like a tropical lagoon, a coral reef, a sailboat. Then there are zoophiles. Are you ready for this? If the following doesn't prove that I know what I'm talking about when I say I'm on the wrong planet... if it doesn't prove that this Planet Earth is full of sickos, then I'm ... I'm... I'm... I don't know what to say. In Washington State, in a picture-perfect corner of rural King County, sheriff's investigators uncovered a nasty little mess: Men having sex with animals at a small farm outside of Enumclaw. The happenings at the farm made Michael Vick's dog fighting ring look like an Amish Sunday picnic. On weekends, Kenneth Pinyan, plus another unidentified man, often visited the farm to engage in sexual intercourse with horses. Yes... Google it if you don't believe me – these sickos were hot to trot. One evening during the "man-horse" orgies, Kenneth died of peritonitis due to perforation of the colon after engaging in receptive anal sex with a horse. Yes... Google it if you don't believe me. In other words.... the horse screwed a receptive Ken – not the other way around (that's the way I read it anyway). The horse, an Arabian stallion, was nicknamed "BIG DICK." No pun intended on my part, that was actually the horse's nickname. The medical examiner says the death was accidental. Well, at least the "horse's ass" Ken is dead, not the horse. According to the award-winning documentary on the case titled "ZOO", Big Dick was castrated. It just doesn't seem fair.

"Living with idiots is like a chronic disease, it's painful but you learn to live with it."
– Barefoot Man

P.S. HELL AWAITS YOU

If it is at all questionable whether or not there is a Heaven, I certainly hope there is a Hell. I know of many that need a reservation for the underworld. The ultimate low-life nut-jobs on Planet Earth are the parents who'd rather pray than take their sick child to a hospital for medical treatment. They are too ignorant to admit that this "praying thing" just isn't working and soon the child ends up in a coffin.

In Weston, Wisconsin 11-year-old Madeline Neumann died March 28, 2008, of a treatable form of diabetes. The girl's mother said, "We believe in the Bible and that healing comes from God." Doctors figure the poor child suffered symptoms of vomiting, nausea, excessive thirst and loss of appetite before she died. While their child was deteriorating in front of their eyes the Neumanns didn't even open a bottle of aspirin... they just prayed until she passed. While police were investigating the matter, the Neumanns remarked that they were not concerned about the investigation "because our lives are in God's hands." In God's hands? Well, if it were in my hands I'd take a crucifix and beat the sh**t out of them. Damn, I'm on the wrong planet. Just think about it... how brain-dead can these imbeciles be?

Another case is where a 14-year-old boy died of a urinary tract infection while his parents refused to take the child to a hospital. Can you imagine how that child suffered? Yes, I hope there is a Hell. Satan, if you're reading my book, hold a seat for these idiots. I'll pay for their first-class tickets.

Ava Worthington was only 15 months old when she died of bronchial pneumonia and a blood infection. This could have easily been treated with antibiotics. Instead, her parents, Carl and Raylene, decided to pray. Forget 9-11, forget the doctors, the Worthingtons forgot to turn on their brains – after all, they had the power of prayer. The Worthingtons belong to the Followers of Christ's Church, a fundamentalist sect that is said to have some 38 medical-denied children lie in their church's graveyard in Oregon City, Oregon. State laws and religious rights often keep prosecutors from charging these religious fruitcakes. However, in a rare turn of events, the Worthingtons were charged with manslaughter and criminal mistreatment. But this Coherent is not impressed. Carl was found guilty and got six months along with six months probation. His wife was NOT charged at all. I wanna barf all over the lawmakers and judges. Just think about it: are your kids getting on your nerves? Just move to Oregon, join the Followers of Christ's Church, then accidently-on-purpose poison your kids. When the police arrive, tell them they accidently swallowed pesticides and you were just waiting for God to heal them rather than call the ambulance. Now, don't forget to hold onto a Bible for the full effect. Six months later you're free of your offspring; no more child support. What a sick, sick planet I'm stuck on. On Planet Coherent, the same day they bury a child who has been denied medical treatment, they also bury the parents – alive, and with their Bible. Let's see if the power of prayer works when you're six feet under. I know there are some readers right now who are saying I've gone too far, I've crossed the line. Well I'll forgive you... after all you are an Earthling and I'm on the wrong planet.

"At least two thirds of our miseries spring from human stupidity, human malice and those great motivators and justifiers of malice and stupidity, idealism, dogmatism and proselytizing zeal on behalf of religious or political idols."
– Aldous Huxley

PARENTS AND CELL PHONES

Family values have gone down the toilet on Planet Earth and who's to blame? The parents, of course. When I sit in a restaurant or on a long flight and note a couple of brats running around tables, through the aisles, crashing into waiters and stewardesses and throwing French fries and ice, it takes a lot for me not to walk over and give them a good whack across the head – I mean whack the parents, not the kids. After all, they are responsible for the snotty-nosed terrorists. Parents with zero ability to raise children should not be allowed to have children.

On Planet Coherent children are not banned from restaurants. It's just that when they are in a place where adults gather, they must behave like an adult, which is difficult – if not impossible for a child to do. So, what's the answer? Simple: just eat and shut-up! When we take you to Chuck E. Cheese or McDonald's then it's your turn to be a kid, run around, spill your sodas and throw your pizza. Then scream to irritate those around you, and if the grownups don't like it – too bad. This is your domain. On my planet it's against the law to impregnate or be impregnated without first attending UPCP (The University of Proper Commonsensical Parenting). Should you care to start a family after your 21st birthday (you must be 21 to knock-up, impregnate or be with child – it's the law) you're expected first to go through nine months of harsh, painstaking parenting classes. You will be taught to dispose your nasty pampers in a wastebasket instead of on the beach. You will be taught to read to your children, to take your children fishing, to not swear, fight or use that four-letter word that starts with "F" in front of your children. You will be taught the rules, regulations and laws of proper parenting. Example: if your 16-year-old steals a car, your 16-year-old will be locked up for a certain amount of time (six months to a year for the first offence). He or she will be locked away in a prison cell with one other prisoner. That other prisoner is you – one of the parents. There will be no cell phones, no TV, no video games, no magazines... nothing except three squares a day (bread and water and vitamin pills) and a belt for the parent. The parent can choose what to do with the belt. You can hang yourself for raising a thief or you can give your punk kid a good trashing every day till you get out. And before you do get out, the parent is responsible to pay for any damage caused to the stolen car. You can't afford it, you say, because you've been locked up for six months! Too bad. We will have your paycheck deducted every week until damages are paid for – you will pay for your offspring's misdeeds. You are the parent. You donated the sperm, or you received the sperm, so you are responsible. I am sure in the future your child will reconsider before stealing again – that is, if you were a proper parent and put that belt to good use.

Pittsburg, Pa. Nov. 4, 2012 – A mother attempts to give her two-year-old son a better view of wild African dogs (so she says). She stands (not sits) her two-year-old on a railing at the edge of a viewing deck. Mysteriously, the kid falls into the pack of the dogs and you know the rest. Why do I say mysteriously? Well let's just think about it for a second. How is it possible for that toddler to fall down 14 feet if the mother was holding onto him as she should have been? Did a tornado come along and tear the child out of her hands? NO! Did the railing break and the child slipped out of her hands? NO! Did someone rip the child from her arms and toss him to the hungry dogs? NO! Was she stupid? YES! The incident came up at our local pub as TV reporters repeated the story for the one-hundred-and-twentieth time. The reaction of the patrons who were gathered for happy hour was the usual Earthling response: sympathetic, pathetic, feeling-sorry-for-the-mother. "Poor mother"..."blah- blah-blah" ... "Sue the zoo." Not one person held the irresponsible mother accountable for child neglect. If it wasn't child neglect, there could only be one other answer – "intentional". Now I'm not saying it was intentional. I was 2,600 kilometers south when this happened on Sunday, Nov. 4, 2012. But for a common sense-thinking Coherent there is something wrong with this picture. Lt. Kevin Kraus of the Pittsburgh police said the attack happened after the mother picked the child up and put him on top of a railing at the edge of a viewing deck. "The two-year-old lost his balance, fell down off the railing into the pit, and he was immediately attacked by 11 dogs," Kraus said. "It was very horrific." This ghastly incident had to be intentional or neglect; one of the two. You choose, and whatever you decide it still makes the parent a moron. If you are walking with your two-year-old along a busy highway, you hold on to him – real tight. If you are walking your two-year-old along a dock, you hold on to him – real tight. If you are dumb enough to stand your two-year-old on a railing to view 11 wild, hungry, carnivorous dogs, you hold on to him – real tight. This type of situation releases the brainless adults that should be tossed to the dogs. "They should put all the wild dogs down," said one blogger. Why should an animal be punished for the stupidity of a human? I am on the wrong planet. Anyone with an ounce of brains would know not to put their children on a railing that overhangs a wild animal habitat. Even "Jacko" Michael Jackson had enough brains to hold on to his child when he did the kid-dangling trick in Berlin. Zoo official Barbara Baker acknowledged there were no warning signs on the enclosure railings. Who needs a warning sign to notify that putting your hand in a fire will burn you? Oh no, lawyers must be beating the parents' door down to get their hands on this case. I can just see it:

Lawyer – "Your honor, the zoo failed to put up warning signs that said, DO NOT PUT YOUR CHILD ON THE RAILING BECAUSE THERE ARE DANGEROUS ANIMALS BELOW."

Judge to zookeeper – "Were there warning signs near the wild dog exhibit?"

Zookeeper – "No sir. Nor do we have signs in the bathroom that read, DON'T DRINK FROM THE TOILET."

One reporter asked Baker whether she took responsibility for not creating a fail-proof exhibit. Such stupid questions piss me off. Why should the zoo be responsible for someone else's lack of reasonable thinking? Why didn't the mother jump over the railing and fight off the dogs, throw rocks, sticks... kick and scream? On Planet Coherent that mother's tubes would be tied and she would get a five-year sentence of feeding wild dogs, gators, lions and rattlesnakes. This would be payback for all the stress she put the zoo through and for the death of her child and one of the wild dogs. Some people should never be parents. Remember when President Obama informed schools that he was going to give a speech to all the children, a speech to perk up their enthusiasm about getting a good education, and to make them feel good about the importance of going to school? The speech was a good thing, yet some lame-brained parents took issue with this perfectly reasonable pep talk. "How dare he use his office to indoctrinate our children? How dare he make kids into pawns in the pursuit of his socialist agenda! This is like Nazi Germany all over again!" they screamed. As I said earlier, I'm not a democrat or republican... in fact I am not even a citizen of the USA, but to protest against anyone giving children a spirit-boosting talk on something as important as education... well, my friends, I am not going to tell you the punishment for these bored soccer moms on my planet.

On my planet all school children, from the time they enter elementary till they leave high school, wear uniforms. All children attending school are well groomed. If you come to school looking like a bum your parents are called to pick you up. No cell phones allowed, no iPods, no smart phones, no guns. Disrespect your teacher? Get ready for a major whack. And when you get whacked, your parents cannot come and defend you. If they interfere, they get whacked also and both of you are expelled from school. Oh, I love that word "whack".

Mandatory school uniforms promote equality and a sense of community so students can focus on schoolwork rather than trying to become a campus status symbol. I recall in my school days the ugliest, pimple-faced high school quarterback was popular because he was on the football team and wore the latest style. Yet the prettiest girl, who happened to be poor and outdated in fashion, was ignored by the cheerleaders and the so called "in-crowd". There are some people on Planet Coherent who will argue against school uniforms – they go so far as to say that forcing children to wear uniforms hinders creative abilities and limits personal expression. What a bunch of crap! Then again, we must forgive them – they have been misplaced and should be on Planet Earth.

Every now and then I need to exercise – so I get out of my hammock, walk into the house and turn on the TV. The other day I did just that and was rewarded with one of the best scenes from a mediocre movie. A Hollywood agent and his movie star client were sitting on the deck of a seaside restaurant. The movie star was in a very agitated mood attempting to explain his dissatisfaction concerning a part he was to play in an upcoming film. Just when it seemed the actor was making his point, the agent's cell phone would ring and the movie star's rant would be interrupted. Once the agent's call ended, the movie star continued his lecture and, once again, before he made his point, the Blackberry would ring and the agent took another call. Well, after this incident repeated itself for the fifth time the actor was so perturbed he snatched the cell phone from his agent and threw it in the sea below.

Wow, I loved that scene. I fell off the couch in laughter. Why? Because I've always wanted to do that. This Planet Earth has gone cell phone mad. Tellers, cashiers, ticket agents – even doctors – have cell phones stuck to their ear while they make an attempt to conduct business.

"Hey, Doc, here's my urine sample, what should I do with it?"

"Oh, just hold on to it and wait outside with the other patients while I take this call from my travel agent."

Damn, that pisses me off!

I've seen police chatting away on their cell phone in their air-conditioned cruiser while some idiot driver runs a red light. They pay the careless driver no mind; they are oblivious to the danger... they are talking on the cell phone. Now, don't try to convince me that they're discussing police business on that cell. Their unconcerned smirks and carefree chatter make it obvious that they are not handling an emergency. That pisses me off! And what about that contraption attached to some people's earlobe while they converse to the atmosphere? Cell phones are OK in the right places, an amazing invention, but why use them in a cinema? During one of my performances at a restaurant I once noticed an entire family – mom, dad, two sons and a grandmother – all sitting together and all five of them texting between chomps and munches. Not once did they look at each other or speak through the entire dinner, except to communicate with the waiter. No wonder good old-fashioned family values are going to hell.

When it comes to cell phones, my Jamaican helper is amazing. She can talk on the cell (without the ear contraption) iron my shirt and work the remote control to our TV – all at the same time. She only does this when she thinks I'm not looking; she knows her cell-jabber irritates me, especially when she's on my time. My teenage daughters refuse to believe my true childhood recollection of when I would beg my mother for a dime and then walk two city blocks to the A&P grocery store to call my girlfriend on the rotary telephone located in a urine-stink phone booth. My daughters can't imagine a planet with no cell phones. She can text faster than I can think, she continually informs me that I'm on the wrong planet. This assessment of her father is correct – I am on the wrong planet, for on my planet, all personal cell phones and other texting devises would be outlawed in the workplace. And all company cell phones would be programmed to handle only company business. I have a suggestion on how government can work more efficiently and save taxpayers' money – take away all civil servants' personal cell phones while they are working on our time. No disrespect intended, but let's not forget they work for us – the taxpaying public.

I also believe that radiation from cell phone overuse will fry your brain. Think about it: nearly every kid in elementary, high school and university has a cell phone and most graduate with a third-grade mentality. Many can't even find America on an atlas. My stance on dense, cell phone-addicted kids once got me into a heated discussion with a close friend.

"My son has a cell phone and an iPad and he's not stupid," he said.

He pulled his teenage son away from a video game. "Son, go bring an atlas from my office and show my friend here where America is located on Planet Earth."

The youngster looked baffled and then asked his father, "What's an atlas?"

To further my point, look at the music kids (and some grown-ups) are listening to these days. There is no rhyme, no tune, no octaves... just repetitive "bass, boom, boom" mixed with vulgar, racial lyrics. One's brain must be fried from cell phones in order to enjoy these noteless, tunlless lyrics.

Technology has made amazing leaps since Columbus's day. Back then a letter from England to Spain would travel for a year before it made it to the addressee. Can you imagine what could have happened when Columbus asked Queen Isabella for finances to discover the New World? The queen certainly would have asked what guarantee does she have that Columbus was not sailing off on some holiday.

"Captain Columbus, how will you know where to go to find the New World? What if you drop off the end of the Earth?"

"Your majesty – I brought for you a smart phone. Just like mine, it has a GPS. We can keep in contact, I can send you pictures."

"A what?"

"A smart phone – it's the latest, hottest item on the market."

"Here, your majesty, take this – it's an Apple iPhone. I will call you daily and send you pictures of the New World."

"You are going to call me, send me pictures on this thing you call an Apple?"

"Yes your majesty... let me show you how it..."

"Show me nothing... Columbus you are a witch... guards... hang him!"

And then what about those grown-ups, those well-educated folks who stand in line at a Best Buy store for eight days just to get their hands on the latest smart phones? What's with that? They already have a perfectly good, working smart phone (often several of them) but the new one has a larger screen and thinner body, so they camp out in wind, hail and snow to get their hands on this latest gadget before their friends do. The new phones can range from $199 to $399.99, yet they take time off from work, pay someone to hold their place in line so they can go piss and buy a $6 cup of coffee from Starbucks. What's wrong with these Earthlings? Why not wait another week and skip the hassle? I asked a close (very smart phone-savvy) friend: "Why? Why do people do that?" His sarcastic response to me went as follows: "They probably still use rotary phones on your planet." Not so, on my planet we are just as advanced in technology as planet Earth. We can, however, wait a few weeks to purchase the latest model. And no one, I mean no one, would ever pay $6 for a cup of coffee.

Do I have a cell phone? I sure do. But please don't leave me a message; I don't know how to retrieve it. Please don't text me – why type when you can talk? And please don't call me 'cause my battery is dead and I can't find the charger.

"I fear the day when the technology overlaps with our humanity. The world will only have a generation of idiots."
– A. Einstein

ANNOYING SPORTS PARENTS

Sporting games can bring out the best in children and the worst in their parents. I hate some of these parents. I want to take the nearest baseball bat and WHACK these idiots across the head – parents who attempt to control every movement their child makes on the ball field. I'm sure you've heard these loudmouth sperm donors before.

"Steal that base!"

"Hit it over the fence!"

"Pay attention!"

"Don't hold the bat so low!"

"Slide, Slide!"

"Use a different bat!"

I can just imagine what poor little Johnny is thinking: "Shut the f #% k up dad, get a life."

It's grueling listening to these parents. Many years ago when my sons played softball there was always such a nuisance in the bleachers.

"Tuck your shirt tail in."

"Let him walk you."

One day I couldn't take any more. I walked up to the guy and told him that I'd seen someone releasing air from his car tire. He rushed off the field and returned 15 minutes later.

"Hey, what's going on? My car is perfectly fine," he says.

"Don't you have a blue mini-van?"

"No I have a blue SUV Lincoln."

"Oops. Sorry, my mistake."

He went back to his seat and the first thing out of his mouth was, "Keep your eye on the ball, it's coming your way." At this point his son was sitting in the dugout and the father never realized it. Oh well, the tire prank did earn me 15 minutes of enjoying the game.

I also hate stereotype sports moms; they are another thorn in my backside. Her son is the worst player on the team, he hates the game, yet he is forced by his parents to play. She shouts out at him:

"That was a good try."

"Don't worry about it; you'll hit a home run next time"

"That's OK, mama loves you."

I can just imagine what poor, little embarrassed Timmy is thinking. "Shut the f#%k up mom, get a life." Most parents mean well, unfortunately they just don't grasp how irritating they are to someone on the wrong planet.

Then there are some parents who are outright insensitive. They humiliate their kids to tears. They are usually huge fans of some professional team. They wear their favorite team's jersey, their cap is on backwards and, through their child, they are playing the game. They shout at the coach and swear at the umpire and, worst of all, degrade their kids and those on the opposing team.

"Kick his ass son."

"Don't worry boy, you can outrun that sissy."

"They should all be on the girls team."

Oh do I hate those infantile adults and feel bad for their kids. I just want to stand up and shout: "It's a game you fool... a game! So shut the f #%k up."

I want to, but never have; usually these masculine dads are bigger than me so I just walk out into the parking lot and flatten their tire.

FADS

One who follows a temporary fashion, notion or manner of conduct exposes themselves as a copycat, the unoriginal. I've always been a non-conformist, anti-follow fashion fanatic. In my high school days everyone was smoking pot to be cool. I never touched the stuff. Now if smoking pot would not have been cool or considered square, I more than likely would have grown weed in my backyard.

"Why do you wear the brim of your hat in the back?" I ask.

"Because I want to be different," the young teen responds.

"But you aren't different. It's a fad. You are plagiarizing what everyone else is doing."

The young man gives me a long bewildering gape before he responds.

"You're on the wrong planet old man."

How did he know that?

I thought they were aliens, extraterrestrials from another planet. Penguin-like, they wobbled through the aisles of Wal-Mart. Their feet faced sideways instead of forward, their legs seemed to be too short for their height. What on Planet Earth were they? They were Earthlings following the ridiculous fashion known as "sagging" or "jailing". Their underwear was more apparent than their drooping pants and they spent more time tripping than moving forward. Sagging can be taken as an expression of rebellion. Men may wear their pants low to prove that they don't amend to rules or care what others think or they could be non-conformist. Oh, no! I'm a non-conformist.

It seems this senseless fashion originated in prison. Why would a free, law-abiding citizen want to dress like a criminal? Ask one of these clowns why they intentionally want to spend their time constantly pulling up their pants; the usual response is they think it's cool. Well it might be cool for a penguin that walks around in the cold all day, but for any human, no matter what your race, it's a moronic fashion. Apparently several incarcerated sources within prisons also consider sagging as absurd. Behind bars it's a way of signaling to other criminals that they are available. In other words, the draggy pants are worn when you are looking for a prison bitch. This notion has often been well publicized in print or the Internet, yet the saggers keep sagging. Then again, when you consider that most of these lame brains can't read in the first place, it starts to make sense. Rap superstar Eminem wears a variety of baggy and saggy pants and jeans which usually reveal his boxers, yet he's a free man, not behind bars. He makes millions of dollars, yet he wants people to see his boxer shorts. Go figure? Then there's the ripped jeans trend. There's something ridiculous about these extreme cases of mutilated jeans. They give the impression that the slashes are for venting, but why wouldn't you just wear shorts or a skirt if it was a hot day?! What a about the bunny ears fad? The ears stick up about 20 to 30 centimeters off your head. What's with that? Tell me guys; would you walk into a restaurant with some dunce wearing bunny ears? Do you find this attractive? It's so silly, unless you're with a Playboy bunny; at least she has the cute little puffy tail to go with it. For about $400, you can buy Louis Vuitton ears and look like an Easter bunny on crack.

JET SKIS

I'm going to paint you the picture. I had just dropped anchor off a remote island in the Bahamas. Not another soul in sight, and the water was so clear it seemed like my boat was floating in air. The palm trees swayed with the southeast trade winds. There was just the two of us. Myself and a lovely young bikini-clad lady (a decade younger than I) were frolicking in sun, sand and sea. At my prompting she had already consumed a half bottle of Dom Perignon (women's Viagra) which was chilling in my cooler. It was a hard task but I finally convinced her to remove her top. Ahh, what a lovely sight – real live, natural, non-silicone boobies. My wife has always been the reserved, shy sort of gal, so to get her to remove her top in the wide open spaces was quite an accomplishment. Now let's work on the bottom.

"Want some more champagne honey bunny, sweetie pie?"

"Well, maybe just a little."

I swim to our boat to retrieve her bubbly and then **–VAAARROOOMMMMMM!**

"What in the hell is that?"

A f***ing Jet Ski! I hate f***ing Jet Skis! I might even hate them more than leaf blowers. On it sits some spoiled brat who got the f***ing Jet Ski for Christmas or birthday or bar mitzvah or just because he wanted it. He shoots by 10 feet from us, just barely missing my half nude honey. She puts her top back on and the wake of the Jet Ski knocks the bottle of champagne out of my hand. Well, there goes my day of Casanovaing out the bilge pump.

I was pissed...

Jet Skis are unpleasant, irksome, noisy additions to any lake, pond or ocean. They give the people who ride them a thrill but annoy everyone else with their irritating whining noise, sounding like an invasion of giant mosquitoes. Jet Skis are not only annoying, they're dangerous, striking swimmers and divers and threatening canoes, kayaks and romanticists about to romance. Jet Skis ruin habitats, smash wildlife, spill Dom Perignon and pollute our rivers, lakes and marine coastlines. Jet Skis also contribute to high gasoline prices, guzzling gas at the rate of one to five miles per gallon. They spew carbon and other filth into the air, contributing to global warming for no other purpose than to allow fools to go around and around in circles, making big waves. I guess Jet Skis serve a purpose as a rescue boat for surfers. I've seen them used often on the north coast of Hawaii. But when you think about it, I'm sure the crash of those 30-foot waves drown out the noise of the Jet Ski.

Besides spoiling passion near a remote island a Jet Ski can also spoil a good day of fishing. Mostly, I've never had a bad day of fishing; whether I catch nothing or fill up my bucket... any day fishing is always a good day. That is until some idiot shoots by in a Jet Ski and scares off my fish, rocks the boat and spills my beer. It's happened to me on several occasions, but on this particular day, the incident was to some extent different.

One day, just on the backside of the reef in Grand Cayman, I was puffing on a Montecristo #2, a cold beer in one hand and hand line in the other. Life was glorious.

PUTTTTERRPUTTTTERRR... What in the hell was that?

It was a Jet Ski. You already know how much I hate Jet Skis but this was different. This Jet Ski was unmanned, slowly moving in the direction of Jamaica. Then I heard voices coming from the inside of the reef.

"Mr. George, Mr. George ...our Jet Ski, our Jet Ski...it got away from us please bring it in."

The Jet Ski was a meager 20 yards away. I could have easily got it.

"What? What? I can't hear you," I bellowed in return. (I heard them clearly.)

"The Jet Ski... there behind you... turn around... please bring it back."

I knew these boys well, they lived nearby and I'd spoken to them often about running their Jet Ski near my beach home disturbing my peace. They were always tinkering with the Jet Ski which they built from parts of other damaged Jet Skis. Any time you ride a Jet Ski and fall off, the Jet Ski is mysteriously programmed to completely slow down and go in circles until you can safely get back on board and continue riding and falling, riding and falling, riding and falling. Obviously this important part of their Jet Ski had not yet been connected.

"What happened to the rider?" I shout. (I was killing time.)

"We fell off, our safety stopper is not working and it went over the reef... please get our Jet Ski."

I pretended to start my small outboard engine, pulling the start chord several times with the choke lever intentionally pulled out. By now, the Jet Ski was nearly out of sight.

"My engine won't start... my engine won't start."

They had now swum back to shore, obviously peeved at me. They gave me the middle finger. I revived my cigar, threw out my hand line and I felt victorious. I had done something good for Grand Cayman – I eliminated one Jet Ski.

One of my daughters, on her seventeenth birthday, requested that I rent her a Jet Ski for an hour so she could join her friends along the beach that ride in circles every weekend. At first I said no, but then I caved in – after all it was her birthday. All the way to the beach toys rental place I preached to her about safety.

"You must wear a life vest."

"OK dad."

"You must stay clear of other Jet Skis."

"OK dad."

"Don't run too close to the shore."

"OK dad."

"You must wear a helmet."

"No way dad. Please, none of my friends wear helmets and it looks too geeky."

Once again, reluctantly I caved in. The shop manager had me fill out several pages of insurance agreements; he took my credit card and asked, "How old is your daughter today?"

"Eighteen." she said hastily.

"No honey, you are 17. How can you forget that?"

On that note he immediately handed back my card and ripped up the contract and made it very clear that she could not ride the Jet Ski on her own until she was 18. However, if I care, she could ride along with me on a double-seat ski.

"What do you think about that honey?" (I knew what the answer would be.)

"No... no... I can't be seen riding around with my dad in front of all my friends, just forget it."

I'm glad she said it first, because I couldn't be seen riding around on a Jet Ski in front of my friends. For once formalities saved the day... for me anyway.

USELESS COMPUTERS

Though I'm an old dinosaur, I love my PC. This book would not be possible if it were not for all the information on Google. My computer also makes me feel better about some of my criticism of Earthlings; because on the Net I have found so many others who think like I do – they must be Coherents. My PC helps me with my spelling and punctuation, though I'm sure any grammar-savvy person reading this book will find its share of typos. I love editing my photos and e-mailing my friends and watching porn. But why put a computer in a stove or a car? My stove will blink and beep and turn off, spoiling my lasagna. The repair man says it's telling me to clean the oven. What? That's none of my stove's business. I curse the stove but even with its built-in computer it's not smart enough to understand me. My mom had an old-fashioned, simple gas stove and when it refused to cook we could quickly pin down the problem – we were out of gas. And what about electric car windows? Who needs them? Why not burn five calories and roll up the window with a hand crank? Then that irritating light that comes on to tell you "check your engine." I pay the mechanic $100 and he finds nothing wrong.

In 2004 we had a major Category 5 hurricane hit Grand Cayman. The island completely flooded and nearly 2,000 cars went out of commission – for good. With their computers submerged in sea-water most of them were indefinitely inoperative. Mercedes, BMWs, Lexus's and fuel-guzzling Hummers were dead. Insurance companies declared bankruptcy and lawyers and judges rode bicycles like a common man. An old auto mechanic told me that had they been built like a 57-Chevy you could have simply washed the engines out with fresh water and went along your way.

They even make computerized cars that will parallel park on their own (no human hands needed) and can do so without damaging the cars in front or behind them. That was impressive to one businessman in traffic-jammed Manhattan, so he purchased a new self-parking vehicle. While in his office, the driver parked behind him rammed into his back bumper attempting to get out of the tight spot. The car's beeper went off and shop owners in the area complained. The police came by and towed his computer-on-wheels to the station and disconnected the electronic beeping irritation. After work, the car's owner noticed there was no car in his parking spot. Later he had to pay $200 to get it out of the police holding yard. As for the damage costs to fix his back bumper...who knows?

My fridge refuses to make ice... something has gone wrong with the fridge computer that makes the ice. So I'm back to the old fashioned ice trays. They always work. On that subject, I am going to mix me a cold margarita and end this chapter.

LACK OF APPRECIATION

"Your attitude will determine your altitude."

I mentioned "appreciation" in the opening of this book. Now, anyone who has read this far without reporting me to the Human Rights Commission, the American Association for the Protection of White People, NAACP, the OCR, Greenpeace or the ACLU, I appreciate it. Let's move on to more things that piss me off.

I have never been a big sports fan. On the rare occasion that I do watch a game at some local sports bar I'll intentionally irritate the customers by shouting out "Touchdown!" when someone hits a home run or I'll ask the bartender to turn on cartoons just when the Super Bowl game is on. Most hard-core sports fans don't find my jests very humorous and, on more than one occasion, I've been asked to shut up or leave. I hold no grudge against those who love their sports. Heck, we even have sports fans on Planet Coherent. However it's those adult Earthlings who paint their faces and trash the stadium parking lot that irritate me. But the ones that really piss me off are the unappreciative jocks who turn into jerks after they sign million dollar contracts.

Many of the individuals on Coherent and Earth work hard. Some even have two jobs and most will never earn in a lifetime what some athletes earn in a week on Planet Earth. Baseball player Alex Rodriguez, during the time of this writing, earned around $25 million a year to hit a ball with a bat. Tiger Woods made over $87 million in 2004 alone. His job is to hit a ball with a club. Michael Jordon made $35 million in one year. His job? Toss a ball in a hoop. Good for them – nothing wrong in making a fat salary for playing with a ball. I'm especially happy for Tiger, who seems like a real down-to-earth guy with no chip on his shoulder (no pun intended).

It's those super-wealthy, ungrateful athletes that really piss me off. They would never have a job in sports on Coherent unless it was to pick up towels and dirty jock-straps in the locker room. Take Tennessee Titans' Vince Young. Six years after entering the NFL as the third player taken in the draft, Vince finds himself nearly broke from a contract that guaranteed him $26 million. Vince and his lawyers have a load of excuses for his financial demise, but at the end of the day, what did he do with all that money? A rough estimate, Vince was making $83,000 per week. That's nearly $12,000 per day. So during the four months "off season", you get up in the morning, have breakfast, later have lunch, later drink beer, later watch TV, go to sleep and then start all over again to spend another $12,000 – INSANE!

Then there's Michael Vick. He made millions to run around with a ball (that was his job). Yes, like Vince he is paid for running around with a ball. Now, where did the millions in his pocket come from? From fans and endorsements. Keep in mind: no fans, no endorsements. Yet this guy gives his fans the middle finger after losing a game to the Saints. He says "up-yours" to the geese that lay the golden eggs. If that isn't enough, there's the dog fighting incident. Vick has had one of the cushiest jobs on the planet (not my planet) and he has the need to be a jerk. Well, he was jerked all the way to prison, minus his contract, endorsements and a huge percentage of his fans. It is said he lost close to $150 million in endorsements. So from superstar to cage – just like the poor animals that are killed and tortured by these insensitive dumb clucks that promote dog fighting. I scratch my head at such stupidity. In 2008 he filed Chapter 11. After he served his time, the once highest paid player in the NFL resigned with the Philadelphia Eagles at $1.6 million for the first year – way too much money in my opinion. As for the cash Vick used to have – his lawyers are grinning from ear-to-ear.

Then there's Plaxico Burress. This Super Bowl hero has to show off his celebrity by packing a gun. When playing with his new toy he shoots himself in the thigh and shot his career in the foot. How brainless can you get? In 2005, he signed a $25-million contract. In 2009, he was sitting in Rikers Island jail being processed for a two-year prison term. Unbelievable Earthlings!

What about golden boy Michael Phelps? An Olympic hero with 14 gold medals earning him millions in endorsements, he was set for life. And what does he do? He puts his cap on wearing the brim backwards, goes to some university frat house, guzzles beer, downs shots and then inhales from a cannabis bong for the world to see. What was he thinking? Hey, don't get me wrong – with 14 gold medals the guy deserves to celebrate. After all, he can't just swim and sleep the rest of his life. But why, why, why with a bunch of loud, obnoxious college students who all have a camera built into their cell phones? " FLASH" goes the cell phone, text goes the cell phone... and before the party is over, Phelps is on the front page of a tabloid sucking on a bong. The media sharks had a heyday. Michael is an adult; he was not competing at the time, so on my planet none of this would have been news or laughed at (except for wearing the baseball cap backwards).

The overall winner of the "DAFT ATHLETICS AWARD" is figure skater Tonya Harding. This air-head Caucasian had a job skating around on ice in a short skirt. She was on TV, signed autographs, competed in the Olympics – she had the world by the tail. There are thousands of young skaters who dream of such successes, yet will never find it. And what does she do? She... she... oh, this story is so ridiculously stupid that I will not waste more ink to write it – except to say Tonya Harding is on the right planet.

On Planet Coherent there are no contracts. Only the athletes that "produce" get the fat checks. In other words, you are paid a very lucrative salary for each game you play. However, if your job is to catch a pass, you'd better catch a pass – or you get deducted for each pass you don't catch. If your job is to throw a pass, better make it on target – or you will be deducted along with the receiver.

"Hey, that's not fair," says the receiver. "The quarterback threw a lousy pass."

Too bad boys. Fight it out in the locker room – you have a cushy job, you make good money and you get a four-month paid vacation. Produce or end up broke. As for bonuses, on Planet Coherent your bonus depends on your fan base. Each fan that buys a ticket chooses their favorite player at the time of purchase. That player gets credited in the accounting system, so if Michael Vick has a thousand fans in the stadium and Palaxico Burress has 800 fans, Michael gets a bigger bonus than Palaxico. However, since Michael gave his fans the finger he gets no bonus. On Coherent he would have been fired on the spot and fans refunded their ticket money. And what's with the guy who runs on the field or the sidelines squirting water or Gatorade in the mouth of hot, thirsty NFL players? What's with that? That pisses me off. Are the players too important or too lazy to get their own water? They make millions and now someone has to bottle-feed them?

No, reader – I am NOT racist or anti-sports, not at all. In fact, all people from Planet Coherent have been programmed to be color-blind – literally. Color and prejudice are never an issue on my planet – however, stupidity is.

"LOVE THY ENEMIES – IT PISSES THEM OFF."

And the idiots keep piling up. Good riddance burglar...

Santiago Alvarado, 24, was killed as he fell through the ceiling of a bicycle shop he was burglarizing. Death was caused when the long flashlight he had placed in his mouth to keep his hands free rammed into the base of his skull as he hit the floor.

Sylvester Briddell, Jr., 26, was killed as he won a bet with friends who said he would not put a revolver loaded with four bullets into his mouth and pull the trigger.

After stepping around a marked police patrol car parked at the front door, a man walked into H&J Leather & Firearms with the intent on robbing the store. The shop was full of customers and a uniformed officer was standing at the counter. Upon seeing the officer, the would-be robber announced a hold-up and fired a few wild shots from a target pistol. The officer and a clerk promptly returned fire, and several customers also drew their guns and fired. The robber was pronounced dead at the scene by paramedics. Crime scene investigators located 47 expended cartridge cases in the shop. The subsequent autopsy revealed 23 gunshot wounds. Ballistics identified rounds from seven different weapons. No one else was hurt.

AND THE WINNER IS...

Zookeeper Friedrich Riesfeldt (Paderborn, Germany) fed his constipated elephant 22 doses of animal laxative and more than a bushel of berries, figs and prunes before the plugged-up giant finally got relief. Investigators say ill-fated Friedrich, 46, was attempting to give the ailing elephant an olive oil enema when the relieved beast unloaded. The sheer force of the elephant's unexpected (expletive deleted) knocked Mr. Riesfeldt to the ground where he struck his head on a rock as the elephant continued to drop 200 pounds of sh*t on top of him.

The stupidity scale keeps rising. How about this for parents with no brains? Two of them named their kid Adolf Hitler. When they attempted to get a cake decorated with Adolf's name on it, the baker turned them away. They also have another adolescent with the middle name, Aryan Nation. These idiots claim they're "not racist" and can't understand why people are appalled. Simply, they are idiots and their poor kids are destined to be bullied and laughed at their whole lives.

AND IT JUST GETS WORSE

Louise Ogborn was 18 at the time while working at a McDonald's in Mt. Washington, Kentucky. She was pretty with a knock-out figure and she worked hard, yet unfortunately she was not too bright. In April of 2004 David Stewart who pretending to be a detective, calls Louise's boss Donna Summers (not the singer of Hot Stuff). He tells her that there has been a complaint filed against Louise where a customer claimed that money was stolen from her purse and that Louise was the culprit.

The make-believe detective orders Donna to take Louise into her office and have her searched. Donna, obviously not being the wisest cheeseburger at McDonald's, followed David's orders. She searched Louise's purse and found nothing. Then she was told via cell phone to have Louise strip-searched. Reluctantly, Louise agreed because she was afraid of losing her job and being arrested for something she didn't do. Again, Donna found nothing. Now let's stop right here for a moment and think about this situation. Donna was the manager of the restaurant, which you'd figure one of such authority would have a smidgen of common sense. However, she believed the guy on the other end of the line was a detective and she figured that it was OK to ask one of her employees to strip. Just when she should have stopped and used her little brain and apologize for the inconvenience, more stupid hormones kicked in. Donna now made a management decision; she called her boyfriend Walter Nix and asked him to keep an eye on the pretty young – and now very naked Louise so she could get back to work.

Walter, who was an exterminator by trade, took on the task. After all, this was a better gig than looking at roaches. Walter continued taking cell phone orders from the phantom detective who asked Walter to have Louise do jumping jacks just in case she had some stolen items hidden in her "you-know-what". Now, let's stop again for a moment... by now Walter, Donna nor Louise had figured out that this was all a prank. What are the odds of three people under the same roof being so daft? And there is more. Louise ended up performing oral sex on Walter – at the orders of the undetectable detective. Now let's stop again for the moment. Louise was naked, Walter was having fun and Donna was serving Happy Meals to customers and between the three of them they continued to swallow David Stewart's prank as if it was a Big Mac with cheese. How stupid can stupid be? The prank finally came to an end when Donna asked the maintenance man to take his turn watching naked, crying Louise. Thomas Simms the maintenance man immediately figured out there was something wrong with this picture... a crying naked teen, an imaginary detective and Nix who had just received a blow job. It took a repair man to out think the three of them. OMG this is an amazing moronic story. Nearly three hours later Donna stuck to her story..."Duh, I thought it was a detective and was doing the right thing." Louise said she was told by her parents to always obey adults. Nix said, "Oh no, I did something bad." OMG... a bag of French fries has more sense than these three put together. Having said all this I honestly feel bad for Louise. I just don't understand how anyone can be so naive. I find it inconceivable to think that the manager of one of the largest chain food restaurants on Planet Earth thought she was doing the right thing. There is a bit of light at the end of this tunnel. Donna was fired, Nix went to prison, Louise sued McDonald's and was rewarded around $6 million (I'd do jumping jacks naked for that) and McDonald's also had to pay $2.4 million in legal fees to the plaintiff's lawyers.

"Stupidity isn't punishable by death. If it was, there would be a hell of a population drop."
– Laurell K. Hamilton, *The Laughing Corpse*

WOMEN WHO LOVE CONVICTS

OK, what is it with these women who fall in love with convicts? Some of the criminals they love are killers, rapists or wife beaters.

Ricardo Leyva "Richard" Muñoz Ramírez was an American serial killer. His highly publicized home invasion crime spree terrorized the residents of the greater Los Angeles area, and later the residents of the San Francisco area from April 1984 until August 1985. Prior to his capture, Ramirez was infamously dubbed the "Night Stalker" by the news media. Ramirez, who was an avowed Satanist, never expressed any remorse for his crimes. The judge who upheld his death sentence remarked that Ramirez's deeds exhibited "cruelty, callousness, and viciousness beyond any human understanding." The Night Stalker raped, beat and shot some 14 victims. His weapons of choice were hammers, guns and carving knives. He was sentenced to death for his crimes. Ramirez was the lowest of low-life killers; he was the bottom of a slime bucket.

Doreen Ramirez disagrees. She says, "He's kind, he's funny, he's charming. He's really a great person. He's my best friend; he's my buddy." He was also her husband. Doreen saw him on television after his arrest for the killings and rape. She began visiting him in prison, sat through his trial and believes to this day that he is innocent. She is well aware that many people think she is crazy or naive.

"Or stupid or lying," she says, finishing the thought.

"And I'm none of those things," she says. "I just believe in him completely."

(OMG... She is about as bright as those poor, wretched folks who give 10 percent of their meager salary to Rolex-adorned televangelists.)

She says she loved Ramirez, and it hasn't come cheap. Her family has disowned her, and she knows she never will have a family of her own.

"I love children," she says.

"I've never made any secret to him that I wanted five or six children."

Thank the Tiki gods that she never had children with Ramirez. Can you imagine six Earthlings roaming around on this planet with "Night Stalker" genes? The thought creeps me out... Doreen creeps me out. Doreen is not alone when it comes to killer pen pals and fans who want to be lovers of killers. But why?

For her 1991 book "Women Who Love Men Who Kill," Sheila Isenberg interviewed 30 women who were married to Death Row inmates.

"Most of these women had been abused in their earlier lives, by parents, fathers, first husbands or first boyfriends," she said. "So a relationship with a man behind bars is a safe relationship. The guy can't hurt them."

Another thing, she added, is that in the pressure to get married, women tend to look for the most macho man around. The guy who pulled the trigger, we tend to venerate the most violent men in our society. By marrying a man on Death Row, Isenberg said, a woman finds a new life that is always dangerous and exciting. Can he make the phone call? Will he be executed? Will he spend 30 years in prison? All these are exciting elements. It's never ordinary.

"It's a very strange world behind prison walls," she said.

It's courtly love, like the Knights of the Round Table. The man in prison has a lot of time on his hands and can romance a woman the way most men can't because they don't have the time. A man in prison can put a woman up on a pedestal and pay attention to her. It's all gentlemanly and formal. The women she interviewed said they didn't have sex (with their imprisoned husbands). It was part of the appeal – it was more exciting to sit at a table, under the watchful eyes of a guard, and just stare.

So just staring at each other under the watchful eyes of a guard is better than having sex? Ramirez – stab me, shoot me, hit me over the head with a hammer. I can't take life on this planet anymore... too many imbeciles. Too late for me, Ramirez can't help. He died of cancer in 2013 – hope it was a slow, painful death.

SOMEONE FELL IN MY TACKLE BOX

Elaine Davidson is the "Most Pierced Woman" according to the Guinness World Records. When examined by a Guinness World Records official in May 2000, Davidson had 462 piercings, with 192 on her face alone. By August 9, 2001 when she was re-examined she was found to have 720 piercings. Performing at the Edinburgh Festival in 2005, the *Guardian* reported that she now had 3,950 body piercings. She has more piercings in her genitalia than in any other part of the body – 500 in all, externally and internally. The total weight of her internal piercings is estimated to be about 3 kilograms. As of May 2008, Davidson's piercings totaled 5,920. As of Feb. 2009 her piercings totaled 6,005. In March 2010, Davidson reported a total of 6,725 piercings. As of March 2012, she had over 9,000. She was born in Brazil and is a former nurse. She does not drink or use drugs. She now resides in Edinburgh, Scotland. On June 8, 2011, Davidson married Douglas Watson, a man with no piercings.

Elaine looks like she fell head-first into my tackle box. Why would she do that? I don't mean accidentally fall in my tackle box, because with beer and rolling sea I've done that myself. What I mean is why would she intentionally stick over 9,000 holes in her body? Why? She is certainly on the right planet. Hundreds of these holes are in her genitalia, and I didn't have to Google 'genitalia' to know where that's located. What was she thinking 9,000 times? She was born in Brazil, so she may have been beautiful before she stabbed herself 9,000 times. Walk down the beach in Rio and you'll know what I'm talking about when it comes to beautiful girls. Some beaches in Rio have become famous because of the influx of beautiful women. With 25,000 people for every square kilometer, the city of Copacabana is persistently packed with many stunning young women. At the beach, you can find the most attractive girls wearing their thin bikinis. Old farts just sit along the side of the beach the entire day and do nothing but stare. I can just imagine sitting on a Rio beach watching all the beauty and there, mixed amongst oily, brown skinned bodies, is Elaine. "Oh and there's my empty tackle box. I knew I left it on the beach somewhere."

Elaine's bio goes on to say that she does not drink or take drugs. Does that mean she stopped drinking and drugging after the 9,000 piercings? How do you drink with 129 piercings in your face? She must gush like a yard sprinkler. She may not drink, but after I saw her photo I had to have a few double shots of rum to get over the sight. And what Guinness World Records official counted hundreds of pricks in her vagina? (no pun intended). To make her claim official, someone had to sit there with a calculator... and... and... yuck! Normally the inspection of this enticing part of a woman's body could be sheer delight. I figure the inspector used a powerful magnet to withdraw the metal while Elaine screamed with delight. And how does she shave down there?

A Coherent, living on Earth, by the name of Tim Pawlenty (former Governor of Minnesota) signed the body-piercing bill into law, which forbid underage youth pocking themselves without parental consent. Considering that parents even need a law proves that body pocking kids are not the problem. It's the parents. They need a good whack for letting things get so out of hand.

The men are just as bad. I've seen them with a beer can wedged through their bottom lip or a large O ring stuck through their nose. A Brahma bull has more sense – the ring in his nose was not placed there at the bull's consent. To make matters worse some of these body slicing humans are covered with tattoos from head to toe. What's with that? A little butterfly or rose tattooed on a shapely girl's butt, ankle or back is acceptable on my planet but to be a walking graphic arts gallery is beyond comprehension, on Coherent anyway. What amazes me is that in most cases the perforated, color-smeared girls are rather pretty when you can see through all the metal and paint. So why do they do that? I got up the nerve to ask a young lady bartender one day. She was pretty, friendly and heavily penetrated with pewter and colorfully coated all over her slim body. She looked directly into my bloodshot eyes and said – "It's none of your fu**ing business." She was right. Beam me up Scotty.

CUSTOMER SERVICE

Just recently I placed a phone call to American Express. I noted from my statement that I had built up around 40,000 reward points. I figured this should be worth something – a free hotel stay, rental car, an air ticket. So I dialed the 800 toll-free number and a robot answers.

"Welcome to American Express – for English press one, for Spanish press two." I press one.

"Welcome to American Express – press one for this, press two for that, press three for membership rewards."

I press three.

"Welcome to American Express – please enter your 16-digit card number."

I enter my 16-digit card number.

"Welcome to American Express – all our customer service agents are busy with other customers. We will take your call in the order it was received."

Next – boring music and boring recorded messages suggesting that I should sign up for the card's membership rewards program.

Twenty minutes later – "Welcome to American Express. This call may be monitored for training purposes."

"Welcome to America Express. My name is Rosita. How can I help you?"

"Yes, I would like use some of my reward points for a hotel stay in Miami."

"Si Señor, what is your 16 digit-card number?"

"I already did that – is this the English language connection?"

"Si Señor – your 16-digit card number please?"

"I punched in the numbers earlier, what happened to that?"

"I don't know Señor."

I verbally repeat my card number and expiration date.

"What was your mother's maiden name?" asks Rosita.

"Why do you need to know that?"

"For security reasons sir."

"I can't remember it and that's none of your business."

"Sir, you gave us this information when you originally applied for your card."

"That was 35 years ago – I can't remember."

She asks me another security question – this time I pass the test.

"OK Señor, I have your record now in front of me and you have 40,000 points, how would you like to use them?"

"How about a hotel stay next month?"

"Sure, you can stay at the Marriott for three nights for your 40,000 points."

"Great – book it."

"You must first call the Marriott's 800-reservation number and get a confirmation number and then call us back with that number so we can send you the proper value in certificates."

"What... I have to call you back?"

"Si Señor."

Damn – that pisses me off!

I hang up and call the Marriott. Fourteen minutes later I obtain a confirmation number. I call American Express back.

"Welcome to American Express – for English press one, for Spanish press two."

And here we go again... the same old, same old repeat of the above. Then 27 minutes later I get a human.

"Welcome to American Express. My name is Roberto. How can I help you?"

"Yes, I want to get a membership reward certificate for a three-night stay at the Marriott."

"Could I please have your 16-digit card number?"

After another 10 minutes of red-tape and frustration, finally they have all the information they need.

"OK sir, what address would you like to use to receive your certificate."

"My regular address – the same address in your records, the same address that I have had for 35 years."

"Oh, I'm sorry – we can't mail these certificates to an address outside of the United States."

"What? Every month for 35 years you manage to get my bill to the Cayman Islands, but now you can't mail my certificates?"

"I'm sorry sir – that's the rules."

"Let me speak to a supervisor right now."

"One moment, sir."

Click – more boring music and more recorded messages inviting me to sign up for their membership rewards program.

Eighteen minutes later – finally.

"Welcome to American Express. My name is Juan. How can I help you?"

"Are you a supervisor?"

"Si Señor, how can I help you?"

"I have a complaint and I am wondering if..."

"Could I please have your 16-digit card number..."

Damn, that pisses me off!!

Over one hour later, I have no rewards certificates, I have a sore throat from shouting and cursing and I have a double shot of white rum in my hand. The whole incident reconfirms – I am on the wrong planet.

On Coherent there is no such thing as a credit card. It's simple: if you don't have the cash to buy it, you don't get it. And don't worry about carrying around a lot of cash. On my planet, robberies are rare. If you rob and we catch you, it's five years in jail – no time off for good behavior, but do add time on for bad behavior. After five years you get out, and now five years' probation starts. No need to check in weekly with your probation officer. However, anytime you leave your home you must wear a loud, neon-colored T- shirt that reads: I'M A SCUMBAG

ROBBER ON PROBATION. If we catch you not wearing the probation shirt, it's back in the can. Anyone who robs another using a weapon or harms someone during a robbery gets the old Islamic treatment: chop-chop, off go the hands. But look at the bright side – on Coherent you will not have to serve jail time after the amputee punishment.

On Planet Coherent, with the exception of private home voicemail devises, all businesses must have humans answering the phone. Not only does this improve customer service it employs millions of people that have been replaced by a machine. We have no separate button for English or Spanish. It's simple. In Coherent's America you get an English-speaking person on the other end of the line. In Coherent's country of Mexico they answer in Spanish. It just makes sense.

Since we're on the subject of Mexico, on Coherent there is no need for U.S. Border Patrol Agents along the boundaries. The solution is simple. Every time we find an illegal Mexican on our side of the border, America will deduct $100,000 from the billions they give Mexico in foreign aid. We are not inhumane on Coherent, so every time an illegal immigrant needs medical care and can't pay the bill, we heal them, deport them and then we deduct the hospital costs along with the $100,000 fine from Mexico's foreign aid account – held in escrow. With that system, the Mexicans would have their own border patrol keeping their citizens south of their border. More than likely Mexico would end up owing us money at the end of a year. Why the bureaucrats on Planet Earth can't adopt this policy is baffling – this idea makes so much sense to me. I have to admit, I can't take 100 percent credit for this clever notion. There are other misplaced Coherents suggesteding the same.

Sorry... really got off the subject there. Back to customer service.

I once went to the Lands and Survey office in Cayman to pick up some documents. I went early to beat the crowd. There were no other customers when I walked in. The civil servant behind the counter was eating breakfast out of a Styrofoam plate – and talking on her cell phone.

"Yes Lucy, I am going to get my hair done after work. Are you going to the dance tonight?"

"Oh, I agree. Isn't he a hunk? Where are you going for lunch?"

"Oh, excuse me miss," I say.

"Take a number," she says.

"A number," I respond. "But there is no one else waiting."

"Sorry, that's the rules. You have to take a number and wait your turn."

I sarcastically check under the chairs, carpet and magazines pretending to look for other customers on my side of the counter in hopes that the idle employee would take a hint or at least giggle at my clowning.

"I see no one else anywhere. Why do I need to take a number?"

Chomping on a piece of bacon she responds, "Take a number!"

I was tempted to jump over the counter and shove the egg sandwich up her backside, but I abstained and walked out doing the best to keep my cool.

Before the door closed behind me I heard her say, "Number one, calling number one." Later I called her supervisor to file a verbal complaint about her rudeness and ignorance.

No one answered except for a voice message that said, "We are experiencing large numbers of calls today. Your call will be answered in the number it was received."

Like family values, customer service has gone down the septic tank on Planet Earth.

On Planet Coherent, grumpy, sulky, lazy, rude individuals simply don't have a job dealing with customers. The Coherent government puts stiff fines on businesses that employ ill-mannered individuals. Of course these crabby cranks are still allowed to work... just not in a job dealing with the public. In fact, on Coherent we have the "GPEA" – The GRUMPY PEOPLES EMPLOYMENT AGENCY. They will fix you up with a "behind-the-door" job, where you can sulk all you want to other irritable equals. And guess what? With the help of the GPEA, everybody's happy on my planet... even the grouches.

MODERN ART

Have you ever seen a famous, expensive painting and said, "Oh, I can do that!" I've seen thousands in my lifetime and most are a waste of canvas and oil – pure mystery to someone like me stuck on the wrong planet. Back in the '60s, artist Andy Warhol painted 32 Campbell Soup cans. He hung the painting up in a museum and he became world famous. Go figure – soup cans? Today, some of his originals are priced in the $400,000 to $500,000 price range. So, just picture it – 32 pictures of soup cans are hanging on the wall of a museum and some snob-nosed critics are examining Mr. Warhol's art.

"Extravagant," says one.

"It has so much depth."

"The color synchronization is spectacular."

WHAT is wrong with these earthlings? It's 32 soup cans – PERIOD. I don't get it!

Abstract art frazzles my brain. For example, a blank canvas with a black dot in the middle. Some museum gives it wall space and some Earthling calls it a masterpiece and then some blind fool buys it for thousands of dollars. Man, am I on the wrong planet. And what about Marcel Duchamp? Now, he was a clever one. He shocked the art world when he took a men's urinal, signed it and displayed it – expert artists tagged it the most influential modern artwork of all time. Now this guy deserves a place on my planet – what better way to piss off a bunch off struggling artists than stopping at the dump to pick up a stained urinal, displaying it and being classified as a genius.

Once, many years ago in Chicago, I went to an art gallery that was hosting a tour of famous works by some of the best-known artists on the planet – dead or alive. I strolled around in amazement, stunned by the display of mish-mash that was guarded by cameras, laser lights and security personnel. I was taken aback by the price tags and, not wanting to be to judgmental, I made a genuine effort to see something within the streaks, strokes and smudges. I was looking for anything, any image that I could extract from the canvas and say, "Oh, now I see it." There were at least 50 framed and unframed canvases, photos and statues, yet the only illustrations in the entire building that had any meaning at all were the silhouette outline of a male and female figure on the public bathroom doors, signifying men's or women's restrooms.

I noted several folks gathered around a picture of what looked to me like spilled paint that someone attempted to unsuccessfully wipe off the canvas. I couldn't resist. I had to ask. "Excuse me folks, not trying to be rude, but what is it you see in this painting?"

"Young man, this is a work of genius by so-and-so." (I forgot the name). "But what is it?" I ask again. "It is whatever you want it to be," said the distinguished-looking gentleman. "OK then, I want it to be a naked girl."

The small gathering abruptly walked away and left me pondering over the image. I eventually gave up, the nude beauty never formed in the confusion of oils and canvas. Obviously I was not only on the wrong planet, I was in the wrong place. An ordinary misplaced Coherent like me should be seeking out the nearest pub instead of critiquing what I can't see.

The incident reminded me of a wonderful time in my life when I spent my days fishing and diving in the crystalline waters surrounding Green Turtle Cay, Bahamas. I was a young lad in my late teens, about to go into my twenties. It was a time when I said God was good on His word when He promised me a happy life to compensate for His mistake of placing me on Earth. Living on Green Turtle Cay at the time was like living in a dream.

Besides the approximately 300 locals who lived here at the time, there were the few tourists and "snow birds or winter birds", as we called them; those who'd spend the entire winter in their second home, cottage or yacht. One of those was a Canadian artist by the name of Jack Gray. Jack spent most of his summers in Canada photographing maritime scenery: the dories, fishing nets, floats and seabirds that made up the Nova Scotia coastline. In the winter he'd cross the Gulf Stream on his yacht, drop anchor off Green Turtle Cay and paint the nautical vistas he photographed. Jack gained fame when President John F. Kennedy purchased his painting titled "Dressing Down the

Gully", which the president displayed in the oval office throughout his reign. Jack's paintings were stunning; there was no mish-mash of perplexing images and colors. He painted a picture that was a picture. You could make out the boats, the people and the lobster traps. There was a sky, puffy clouds and ocean spray so clearly illustrated you could see the salt crystals on the canvas.

Jack was a regular customer at the Green Turtle Yacht Club where I worked; he'd come to dinner, have cocktails and make small talk with other guests. During one evening's happy hour, Jack and a snooty, slightly intoxicated New York art critic got into a friendly disagreement concerning abstract art versus realistic art. Though the critic respected Jack for his success, she did not personally care for Jack's style of painting. In her opinion, abstract art was the only kind of art and Jack was not an accomplished enough painter to do so-called "imaginary art". The discussion ended in a bet. Jack would prove that the majority of abstract art was nothing more than paint sloshed on canvas. It was a simple, fun bet. No high stakes were involved, just a few cocktails.

Jack would paint an abstract, frame it, display it and sell it – that is, if he could sell it. If he couldn't, the art critic would be declared the winner and Jack would have to pick up the bar tab when they met again at the same time, same place the following year. Spring, summer and fall passed and everyone at the Club had forgotten about the wager, but not Jack who had just arrived for his annual winter jaunt. Once the word got out that Jack would exhibit his first-ever abstract painting, a messenger was sent to the far side of the island where the art critic was staying at her winter retreat.

It was an exciting evening – the snow birds came in flocks. The lounge was jammed with the upper crust of the island, all wearing their smartest tropical attire: gentlemen with pipes, monocles, ascots and bow ties and ladies showing off their finest jewelry and highest heels. Sipping on martinis and rum punch the crowd gathered around the easel draped in a white sheet. Guarding his masterpiece, Jack made a short announcement.

"Ladies and gentlemen, thank you for showing up this evening. Some of you may have witnessed the discussion between myself and Mrs. Scolley* last winter. It seemed at the time Mrs. Scolley was convinced that I, an artist that paints realistic images, could not paint abstract." The tone of Jack's speech was teasing and jest and the audience (with the exception of Mrs. Scolley) was humored at Jack's mockery of abstract art. With that, Jack unveiled his one and only abstract magnum opus. The room fell into a hush – no one spoke; you could only hear the faint squawking of seagulls on the dock. Soon, someone broke the ice with a polite low-level applause, while others (like me) scratched our heads at the nonfigurative chaos in front of us. Mrs. Scolley was not impressed; she announced that she was still the winner because the agreement was that Jack must sell the painting. "I'll buy it," said one of the inebriated guests. "I'll give you a dollar for it," I said jokingly. "But what is it?"

"It's already been sold," announced Jack, and with that he produced a check from his blazer that was well into the five figures. Jaws dropped, the crowd cheered and I repeated, "But Jack, what is it?"

"This masterpiece is titled "It is What it Is". Over the last year as I've been painting my realistic art I'd clean the excess paint off my brushes on this canvas. The colors mounted and mixed, jumbled and drained and when I was done I simply framed it and signed my name to it," Jack explained. "So, to answer your question – it is what it is."

For a long time I have attempted to find this painting on the Internet, with no luck. Maybe Jack just tossed it in the dump and maybe the five figure check was nothing more than a sham to humiliate Mrs. Scolley. Jack, like myself, was a misplaced Coherent.

*(Mrs. Scolley is a real person but the name is fictional).

SUICIDE

Over 90 percent of people who die by suicide have clinical depression or another diagnosable mental disorder. Many times, people who die by suicide have a substance abuse problem. Often they have that problem in combination with other mental disorders. Adverse or traumatic life events in combination with other risk factors, such as clinical depression, may lead to suicide. But suicide and suicidal behavior are never normal responses to stress... and these are sad cases – to a certain extent. Worst of all are the young people who commit suicide caused by bullying – what a waste of life just because some punk beats up on someone weaker than him. Shoot bullies.

It is estimated that on Planet Earth over one million people per year commit suicide. They hang themselves, jump off bridges, drink pesticides or blow their brains out. And, I say, what's wrong with that, in certain specific situations. Fewer people, more trees. In any case, the point I am trying to make is if a person is in his right mind, if the person has a terminal illness, if a person can't stand life anymore on this messed up planet, if a person's life has been so good they are afraid of something bad happening, well then ending it all is the individual's business, it's their body and if they want to go – let them go (that's my opinion). So leave them and their body alone, as long as they don't damage property or hurt someone physically in the process of their demise. If I decide tomorrow that I'm going to drink myself to death that's my business – not yours. Man, it pisses me off when I see a news flash where some someone is standing outside his 20-story window and the cops are attempting to change the jumper's mind. They bring in the fire department for help, they bring a huge bouncy castle to break the fall, and they bring in shrinks and priests. Hey, leave the man alone already; if he's an adult and he wants to jump, let him jump for Pete's sake. On Coherent, if you should care to jump off a building, that's cool. Just give us some notice so we can move the cars below and tape off the area so you don't fall on some innocent bystander. We would, however, require a $30 deposit before your leap. After all, someone has to clean up the mess. On Coherent suicides are rare, committed only amongst the misplaced Earthlings who can't take life in a commonsensical society. Now, if the leaders of nations on Planet Earth had as much wisdom as I do, they would take my advice and build a Suicide Amusement Park.

Welcome to KEVORKIAN LAND!!!

This entertainment center, named after the famous Dr. Death, would assure you freedom to "kick the bucket" with no interference from lawyers, police or psychiatrists. Much like Disneyland, Kevorkian Land is divided into separate parks such as "The Jumping Arena". Here, tall buildings, bridges and even a Disney-style Matterhorn Mountain are available for that final leap. There is the "Speeders Arena" where we allow drunken, stupid idiots to put the pedal to the metal and smash into trees, walls or telephone poles. We can even have the police chase you, if you wish. Then there's the "Overdose Theater" with a huge selection of drugs to die for. Just like in Disneyland, there are monorails and old-fashioned-style railroads that take spectators from one park to another. In Kevorkian Land we allow you to jump in front of the trains without any reprimand. All of these grand finale options are free of cost to you because Kevorkian Land is also open to the public who pay an admission charge to watch their favorite gore. Part of the gate proceeds would go to the estate of the departed, who can leave these funds for family or a favorite charity. If you care, your beneficiary can collect additional funds from the sale of T-shirts that display your picture and the date you expired. Kevorkian Land has several gift shops where neat, nauseous souvenirs are for sale.

Another popular spot at Kevorkian Land is known as "The Euthanasia Gardens". This area is closed to the public; here, the suicidal can go in quiet, peaceful surroundings far away from the huge crowds in the other theme parks. The park's highly trained specialists would personally see to your voluntary demise. For an additional cost, The Gardens will provide anything you please on your final days: booze, music, movies, prostitutes and even painkillers for those with a terminal disease. At

Kevorkian Land we will do everything we can to make your last days on Earth pure Heaven. Dr. Kevorkian believed that those suffering from depression, shame, guilt or health problems have a right to end their misery. I agree with the wise doctor. Let me have the right to kick the bucket, rather than have my wife, daughters or some male nurse change my diaper in a state of coma or over-aged age.

Even terrorists would be welcome at Kevorkian Land. They could blow themselves up in "Kamikaze Park" and then be rewarded with 72 virgins and stay forever young when they get to their indigenous heaven. What a great compromise – they could have their virgins, meet Allah and end the killing of innocent people. The only drawback I can see is that Planet Earth is short on virgins. Well anyway, when I think about it, it makes so much sense – 72 virgins and eternal youth are a strong motivation for suicide and I'm sure there are many misguided, young, horny terrorists who are sucked in with this bad theology. Not all are interested in killing innocent people – they just want those young hot virgins. Another plus when blowing yourself up in Kevorkian Land is you don't need to go through the rigorous training in the hot desert – no climbing the monkey bars or the hassle of trying to get your bombs through security. We make meeting your demise easy. Why, the US and Israeli governments would even provide free, first- class transportation for terrorists to Kevorkian Land.

Kamikaze Park is the most popular and profitable of all the theme parks. It is set up like an old Roman coliseum where the audience cheers and jumps with glee at the big bang. For a realism effect, the terrorist can choose from a variety of stage sets, which include backdrops of restaurants, airplanes, buses or even a marketplace. And, for those older, more unfaltering terrorists who insist on killing a few people, Kevorkian Land will provide a few of the worst death-row inmates at no extra charge. The older I get, the more I think about those 72 never-before-copulated beauties. If I had some guarantee that this "72 virgin myth" was, in fact a fact, I'd properly blow myself up. I know what you're thinking... I'm on the wrong planet.

"On Planet Earth - The Supreme Court has ruled that they cannot have a nativity scene in Washington, D.C. This wasn't for any religious reasons. They couldn't find three wise men and a virgin."
– Jay Leno

THE PRESS

I believe in freedom of the press – media is a good thing. However when you consider that most tabloids outsell responsible publications it only proves to me that I'm on the wrong planet. Only an Earthling could believe and buy a newspaper with such headlines as "Holy Water Cures Cancer"; "Aliens Kidnap Babies in Romania"; "Catholic Priest Molests Altar Boys" – well, the latter was actually true.

On Planet Coherent only the misplaced Earthlings buy this trash. Considering there are so few of them, the demand for tabloids is little. Coherent's No. 1 selling paper is the *Rational Enquirer*, where headlines are much different.

"Catholic Priest Is Castrated By Enraged Parents"; "Holy Water Poisoned"; "The Barefoot Man Voted Sexiest Person Of The Year" – well, the latter is actually false.

My favorite headline of all time was: $1,000 Reward for Burger King Robbers. This appeared in the Cayman Islands July 26, 1984 edition of the *Caymanian Compass*. Though, at the time, I was saddened that such a thing could happen in the blissful, crime-free Cayman Islands, the illustration that went with the front page story had me rolling on the floor with laughter. The article featured a police artist's composite of the hooded robbers. Yes, I said "hooded robbers". The dim-wit police artist drew an image of what looked like two paper bags on the robbers head, with holes cut out for the eyes.

"So, can you give me a description of the robber's facial features?" asks the detective. "Well, they had a paper-like look," says the Burger King manager.

"Mmmm. So how would you describe the shape of their face? Long, oval, square?"

"I guess square."

"How about their hair and eyes?"

"Well, I saw no hair and only two holes where the eyes should be."

The detective scribbles, erases, and then doodles some more.

"There, how's that? Does that look like them?" The detective drew his idea of what a paper bag would look like.

"Wow! That looks exactly like them," says the manager. "Very impressive."

"That's what they pay me for," the detective proudly says.

So, there it was on the front page for all to see, a drawing of two square paper bags with cut-out holes for the eyes. The police were requesting that the public take a good look at the illustration. "Look out for these robbers! Can you identify these robbers? Anyone having information on their whereabouts please contact the police." Now, the Keystone cop's composite drawing was one thing, but the fact that the newspaper published it only validates – I'm on the wrong planet! This was big news on the island. The rare robbery and paper bags with arms and legs were featured on the front page. I studied the artist's impression very intently. After all, I wanted that reward. I mean, $1,000 is a lot of money for a poor beach bum. The next day I played bounty hunter and drove all over the island looking for two people wearing paper bags over their heads. I had no luck.

One more irritation since we're talking about the media. " Boring celebrity news" , why ? Who cares if some model is wearing $ 2,000 pair of shoes or that baby George "blew bubbles while Prince William bounced him."

Are there people out there that really want to know this stuff? Kate Middleton's stunning post baby evolution, see what celebrities are dressing as this Halloween, Tom Brady buys $ 14.million dollar condo (who's Tom Brady)? Here's a fresh one, Professor uses camera pen to prove students not wearing underwear. MMMMMM that one is worth checking out.

Oprah has yard sale, what? Who gives a crap? I'm sure that most celebrities are embarrassed when the media exposes what type of cereal they prefer for breakfast or how much money they spend on their sunglasses. As I'm writing this section I talk to my dog named "Cat" – "what do you think Cat; give me your opinion on this uninteresting, tedious celebrity news." Cat walks over towards a bush and takes a dump. Message understood.

"Two things are infinite, the universe and human stupidity, and I'm not sure about the former."
– Albert Einstein

PIGS IN A BEACH BLANKET

Is there really such a place as Planet Coherent? I can't confirm that, since I've never been there. However, if there is a paradise I think I've found it here on Earth; Big Majors Cay.

Wanderlust has my passport in shreds. I've traveled to the Cook Islands to hang out with pearl divers in a Manihiki lagoon; to Ireland to sleep in castles; and to Molokai to visit a leper colony. However my trip to Big Majors Cay earns a top spot in the "damnest thing I've ever seen."

The Exumas are a chain of islands stretching for some 120 miles in the Bahamas. There are 365 islands... you can visit a different one every day of the year. There are more powdery white sand beaches than you can count in a lifetime and water so clear it makes gin look polluted. My destination was Big Majors Cay, home of the swimming pigs. Yes, you read right – swimming porkers that live in paradise... pigs in a (beach) blanket. Several of my Bahamian friends told me, "There's nothing there except pigs and a beach, so why go there?" Nothing there! If that means no humans, that's music to my ears. I know a lot of humans that are pigs, so what's the difference.

There's nothing much on Staniel Cay, which offers the only airport in the area, but that's the way I like it. Local artist Bernadette Chambers rented my wife and I a small, cozy cottage and made arrangements for the lease of a 17-foot Boston Whaler. A boat is a must in the Exumas – there are so many human-free islands to explore and it's the only way to get to Big Majors Cay. We had just landed and I was ready to cruise. I rushed my wife to get moving. Always being meticulous, she was inspecting her check list – sunscreen, gas, oil, life vests, camera, etc. The Atlantic side of the islands was blowing 20 knots, yet on our lee side the sea was smooth as polished steel. The water was so clear our vessel seemed to be floating on air. I had a gratifying smile on my face. There's nothing that gives me more pleasure than being on the sea with no specific destination, no plan and no cell phone. I have lived most of my life on tropical islands. I have "beachcombed" with a vengeance, and sought pleasure wherever it is to be found. I have tried hard to stay happy, enjoying a felicity unknown to the average mortal. You might say that is how I survive being placed on the wrong planet.

Within swimming distance from Staniel Cay is Thunderball Grotto. It's nothing more than a huge hollowed-out rock that looks like iron shore from the outside. I say hollowed-out because it's actually a cave and the only way to enter it is to free dive about five feet, swimming amongst thousands of tame, colorful tropical fish waiting for a handout. Once in the cave, it's a sight to see. The ceiling of the cave is dotted with small holes allowing the sunlight to shine through, creating an underwater laser effect. Several early James Bond films and Disney's "Splash" had the honor of filming scenes here. I found the place amazing – an unspoiled natural wonder on a planet filled with mind-numbing inhabitants who would never appreciate the beauty and seclusion of a simple cave.

Back in our vessel, the blazing sun had reached its midday peak and we made our way towards Big Majors Cay.

"Did you bring some food for the pigs?" asks my wife.

"Food? No food... I do have a cooler full of Kalik beer," I respond.

My wife is a devout animal lover so I was firmly instructed to turn the boat around back to Staniel Cay for get some lunch (leftovers) for the pigs, which the Yacht Club gives away to visitors for hog feeding.

From the moment they heard our boat engines, the pigs came running from the bush. There must have been at least 20 of them, in shades of sunburned-pink to tanned-brown. They galloped down their very own private beach – a beautiful beach that most developers would kill for – and then dove into the transparent sea towards our boat.

Swimming porkers! I had no idea pigs could swim. I tried to imagine what they would taste like: sea-salted porkers that waddle in powdery white sand instead of mud; porcines that eat coconuts for dessert; 300-pound swines that swim better than the average tourist. And why aren't the sharks here having a porky buffet? It was all a mystery. I was overwhelmed by it all. Others may say, "What's the big deal... swimming pigs?" Well, I've already said it; I see bliss differently from the average-thinking mortal because, let's not forget, I am on the wrong planet. Let me explain: these pigs are living my dream. They have their own tropical island, they swim and eat in a gin-clear sea, they don't have to wear clothes and they are not ashamed of their obese figure because they don't have to keep up with the Joneses. There are no humans on their private Eden; the few humans who do visit are their servants, delivering leftover steak, lobster and Caesar salad from the Yacht Club around the bay. I've always heard that pigs are intelligent. Well, now I'm convinced.

I was told that there were some 100 pigs on the island including several baby piglets. It seems they come out in shifts. They gorge themselves and then sleep in the shade of a coconut tree while another set of pigs greets the next visitors – and they will gladly pose for a photo in exchange for a discarded hamburger bun or stale potato chips. While my wife feeds the happy pigs, I'm hit with a stroke of resentment and, once again, I question God's deeds. Why would He do this to me? If you're going to put me on the wrong planet at least you could have put me on my own island so I can live out my life without the foolhardy who dominate Earth. Instead, He donates this tropical bliss to a bunch of swines, hogs and boars.

Later that evening in the restaurant I couldn't stop thinking about those lucky pigs. Those gentle, intelligent animals that live in paradise – and once again jealousy got the better of me.

"Sir, are you ready to order? What would you like for dinner?" asks the waiter.

"Do you have pork chops?"

My wife whacks me across the head with her menu.

I made several more visits to Majors Cay before our trip ended. At the tiny Staniel Cay airport we waited for our flight to Fort Lauderdale. My wife, who is always a fidgety flyer, was praying for a safe flight on the small single-engine aircraft. I had a few private words with the Tiki gods myself.

"Please... please...God. If I'm ever reincarnated, I am giving you the OK to place me on the wrong planet, as long as you bring me back as a big fat porker, a citizen of Big Majors Cay, so I can bask in the sun, swim in the Caribbean Sea, be hand-served by tourists... I want to be a pig in a blanket – a beach blanket.

"Animals have advantages over man: they never hear the clock strike, they die without any idea of death, they have no theologians to instruct them, their last moments are not disturbed by unwelcome and unpleasant ceremonies, their funerals cost them nothing, and no one starts lawsuits over their wills."

– Voltaire

"I like pigs. Dogs look up to us. Cats look down on us. Pigs treat us as equals."
– Sir Winston Churchill

AMERICA – WHAT A COUNTRY!

I think that the U.S. Government should give me honorary citizenship. When traveling in America I am constantly verbalizing, "America! Oh, what a country!" I say this not out of sarcasm or disrespect. I truly mean it – what a country!

I'm a Bill Maher fan. Though much of what he says on political issues goes way over way my head, I am impressed with his ridicule of top politicians. He will ridicule the president, demolish Sarah Palin and scorn the Pope. Now, it's not that I always agree with his point of view, but think about it: he gets paid a monster salary from HBO to shame world leaders. It's the pinnacle of "freedom of speech". What a country!

It drives me totally nuts when I visit Miami. In Miami, the billboards are in Spanish, 80 percent of the population talks in Spanish, a large number of the radio stations are in Spanish and it's common to deal with individuals who can only speak Spanish. They can't speak English in America and think they don't need to. America, what a country! Many of these lucky American citizens washed up on Florida's shore in a raft with only the sodden clothes on their back, and now they have homes, cars and freedom. I say, good for them – it proves that if you have no problem with hard work you can do anything you want in America. But please, learn to speak English. This great country has welcomed you with open arms, so the least you can do is speak English. No, no, no... I don't care what you say: I am not a racist. I am just saying, don't be rude. Be appreciative and learn to speak English and consider yourself lucky that you are on Planet Earth because on Coherent's America, you either learn English or it's back on the raft.

With the exception of some misplaced earthlings on Planet Coherent, discrimination just doesn't exist. The unnecessary ranting and ravings of the Jesse Jacksons, Al Sharptons and the KKK are simply ignored by most commonsensical Coherents because it simply makes sense that they make no sense. And, as for those white supremacist Nazi sympathizers, they are deported to the gas chamber to get a taste of their hero's medicine. WHAT, did I say? If you don't get my point, you're an Earthling.

America: what a country of strange regulations, rules and awkward legal requirements. Man, does America love law suits. If you're clumsy enough to spill hot coffee all over yourself at McDonald's you can sue the franchise. One guy sued a strip club because he got a stiff neck watching the strippers – only in America, on Planet Earth. There are endless examples of killing common sense such as the "carding" rule in many parts of America. Here is how I first encountered that:

I was in Nashville, Tennessee, doing some recording for a new album. I was in my motel room watching a dirty movie when I got the munchies. I called the front desk for information on the closest beer and potato chips provider. Two blocks down the road there was a convenience store with everything I needed for the late-night munchies. I also needed a little exercise, so I decided to leave the rent-a-car behind and hike the few blocks.

It turned out to be more like four blocks – but no complaints. I was happy to see the huge selection of beers and high-calorie snacks. I went to the counter to check out my items... Dorado chips, bean dip, candy bars and a six-pack of brew.

"Could I see your ID sir?" says the chubby cashier.

"ID, for what?" I respond.

"The beer sir."

"The beer... you are carding me?"

"That's correct sir."

"Miss, are you playing a joke? I passed 21 over three decades ago."

"Sorry sir, I have to card everyone."

"Miss, I walked down here from the motel four blocks away and I didn't bring any sort of ID."

"OK sir, I'll put the beer back up for you. Would you like a coke?"

"No, I need a beer... I can't watch dirty movies in a Motel 6 without a beer."

"Sorry sir."

Amazing, amazing... who made these ludicrous rules? The same thing happened on the way home at a mojito bar in the Miami International Airport. As I was showing the bartender my passport, driver's licence and birth certificate, a porter pulls up pushing an old man in a wheelchair. This very senior, senior citizen had a walking cane and air tank attached to the seat and a breathing tube stuck up his nose.

"The old man wants a mojito," says the porter. "Make it a double."

"Could I see his ID please," replies the bartender.

Now, who created this brainless regulation? I had to find out. I made several calls to the head office that has the bar franchise at Miami International. What I got was no answer, only a vague, "It's the law – we think."

Another response to my question was, "Hey, that's a good question."

Then, finally I got a bottom-line answer – an answer that made no sense.

"Discrimination," said one of my lawyer friends.

He attempts to explain.

"If they card you and not me, they are saying you look younger than I do – which we all know is not true. So, they are showing favoritism to you by not asking me for my ID."

What a defense. I thought to myself, "only on Planet Earth." I wonder: could the employee who is required to ID a 70-year-old man file a law suit against the company he works for? I put the question to my lawyer friend.

"What are you suggesting?" he responded.

"OK, just hear me out. Think about it, if I was a bartender and my employer says I must card everyone before they get a drink, no matter what age, my employer is telling me that I'm stupid and have no common sense – in fact he is saying that I am so unwise that I can't tell a teenager from a senior citizen. Any slimy lawyer could twist that into a slander or defamation case."

The lawyer's money-hungry eyes light up.

"You know, you could be right – sounds like the makings of a good law suit."

He jotted down the idea on a cocktail napkin.

On a later trip through Miami International I tried a new slant.

"Could I have a double mojito with extra lime."

"I need to see your ID sir."

"Sure, I'll comply, but could I please see your ID first."

The bartender was thrown off guard at my request. He gave me a perturbed glare and repeated his instructions.

"I need to see your ID sir."

"Sure sir, but I need to see your ID also."

This time he rewarded me with a slight grin.

"OK sir, what's your game – why do you need to see my ID?"

"Because it's against the law for a minor to consume or serve alcohol so I need to see your ID in order to make sure you are old enough to serve me since you think I'm too young to drink."

This rendered some giggles from the customers and even the bartender. I was in a bickering mood and enjoying the attention, when the public address system announced that the airport was on a code orange alert and any unattended bags would be confiscated and any suspicious, obnoxious acting person should immediately be reported to the airport authorities. I ended my little farce right then and there and showed my ID. I figured I'd best stop while was behind.

In 1988, Mother Teresa sent two nuns on a mission to New York City to find a cheap abandoned building that could be converted to a homeless shelter. Mayor Ed Koch offered her two fire-gutted buildings for one dollar each. What a deal, our prayers have been answered – praise Mother Mary! As the nuns and the local priest sprinkled holy water throughout their newly-acquired shelter the local building inspector walked in with his clipboard and 200-page regulation book.

"Good Day ladies, where will you place the elevator?"

"Elevator, kind sir – we do not need an elevator and even if we had one we would not use it. We are the Missionaries of Charity and we avoid the routine use of such modern conveniences as an elevator."

"Sorry girls, I have the building code book with me and if you care to see the section on elevators I would be happy to show it to you."

"But sir, the mayor himself donated these building to Mother Teresa. Have some compassion. All we do here is for the poor and homeless, we simply cannot afford two elevators."

"Sorry Sisters... it's the LAW!"

Though there are a thousand buildings in the city without an elevator the law says that any new or renovated building must have an elevator. So to make a long story short, the plan was scratched and the homeless in the area of 148th Street remained homeless and the good-hearted nuns are dumbfounded.

I had my own personal experience dealing with the bureaucracy and pointless regulations of our Planning Department on Grand Cayman. In September of 2004 Grand Cayman was hit by a powerful Category 5 hurricane that destroyed or damaged 80 percent of the buildings on the island including my home, which fell not in the destroyed or damaged category but more in the "washed away" category. Hurricane Ivan skimmed along the south shore of Grand Cayman and my lovely seaside home stood in its path. The concrete walls and hurricane shutters may have stood against the 155mph winds, however against the mighty sea my little home along with 25 coconut trees, didn't stand a chance. Though it was a major stumbling block in my life on this planet, the calamity didn't come as a surprise. After nearly three decades of evading direct hits from monster storms that lurked in the western Caribbean, my time had come. Living in paradise is not free.

As weird as this may sound, the five weeks following the hurricane turned out to be an unforgettably delightful experience. The island came to a halt, and that's how I like islands. Over 10,000 people evacuated and some 20,000 saltwater-logged cars were dead, forever off the road. I managed to get my family off island within a few days after the great storm. Living with three girls who could not shower or do their hair was pure misery. Until the island recovered and I could find a new home, my wife and daughters moved in with family in the US and I was alone: just myself and the sea, a hammock, a BBQ grill and an ocean kayak.

We had a long calm after the storm. For several weeks the sea was a pond and the lagoon was packed with lobster and fish that had apparently been washed in the shallower waters from the deep. During this wonderful time there was no electricity, no computers, no banking to be done, no mail service and no ice. The latter was my biggest challenge. I had my local connections – beer for me was abundant and fresh seafood was plentiful. However, the quest for ice was never-ending until my friends discovered that I was fishing daily and then ice delivery became a norm. We simply bartered: two fish equals one bag of ice, two lobsters equals a bottle of rum and a few conch were traded for a bowl of peas 'n' rice. I became an entrepreneur-ish Robinson Crusoe. Sure, I missed my family – but teenaged daughters just don't mix without AC or running water. For me it was happy time. Attached to our pool, which was now filled with sand and concrete, we have a small 20x20 cottage that we simply call the "pool house", much like an American garage. Before the storm it was used mainly by the children for TV watching or hanging out with their friends. Since this structure was built behind the old house and not in direct line of the sea, it survived the great storm. The main house acted as a barrier – it took the brunt of the 40-foot waves. Once the island got back on its feet, I began the hunt for my insurance agent. I was one of the luckier ones; within a few months I had a check in my hand, and enough money to rebuild. Unfortunately, some were not so lucky. Either they were uninsured or failed to collect from bankrupt insurance providers. I decided to rebuild on my seaside property; I could not imagine living away from the beach.

I presented my architect a simple plan for a simple new home. Four walls, a roof and everything up on stilts so the sea could wash under and around my new home should we have a repeat of such catastrophe. On completion, I hand-delivered my plans to the government planning office and asked them to please rush my approval. By now my family had returned and I was paying rent, which was eating up my insurance pay-out. I had been warned that the wheels of government turn slowly, but I had never imagined that they would move in reverse. Several weeks went by and no word, so I went back to the authorities and started jumping up and down demanding the stamp of approval to build my home. I needed a home and temporary renting in a suburban neighborhood was driving this recluse mad. Time slouched along, then after few more weeks of waiting, I finally received a response. I was asked to meet with one of the planning inspectors. He advised me that my plans were incomplete and not up to the local standard for a residential building.

"You have no kitchen," he says.

"No kitchen... I don't need a kitchen; I plan on using my undamaged pool house as a kitchen."

"Sorry a kitchen must be inside your house," he responds.

"Why?" I shot back.

"It's the rules, I didn't make them. I just have to make sure they are enforced."

Another rule, another senseless requirement. "What if I was a rich man and ate out every night? What if I ordered pizza every night? What if I didn't have any hands and couldn't cook?"

"Sorry, you have to re-do the plans and add a kitchen to the inside of your new home," he repeats.

"I don't want a kitchen. I want a caboose, separate from my house."

Ironically, all the old homes on the island used to have a caboose. The wise old folks figured it just made sense. In case of a stove fire your house wouldn't burn down because your kitchen is not attached to your home. In a new era the bored university-trained experts need something to do, so they sat around with their laptop and created regulations so they could have something to regulate... I'm on the wrong planet. The real madness with such rules and regulations is that in most cases the taxpayer is paying the salary of the numbskulls who create these laws. Someone gives someone a position, an office and a parking spot and they go ordinance crazy.

Did you know that in Alabama it is illegal to be blindfolded while operating a vehicle?

In Alaska, it's illegal to push a moose out of a moving airplane.

In Florida, men cannot be seen in public wearing any kind of strapless gown.

And this is one of my favorites – in Illinois, it is illegal to give a lighted cigarette to cats, dogs or any other domestic animal considered a pet.

What were they thinking when they sat in some boardroom working on the proper wording of these directives? Well, one could argue that these laws make sense in theory, sure – but why make the law in the first place? On Planet Coherent they have one simple law that covers all these pointless laws – it's against the law to be stupid. After much hassle and becoming a total pain-in-the-neck for the Planning Authority we came to an agreement. I was instructed to build a porch-like cover between my new home and the ten-and-half feet to the (pool house) caboose. The cover would attach the two buildings and then the inspectors would let the silly rule slide. This unnecessary delay caused me further expense in material and rent. But why? Why is a kitchen compulsory? I can understand a toilet... but why force me to cook? When the final inspection was done on my home, the building inspector did not even take notice of the additional $1,200 in expense I had nailed to the two buildings. That pissed me off.

Though placed on the wrong planet I am thankful that I live in seclusion. Besides my lovely wife, my dogs, curly tail lizards and the seabirds, I have no neighbors. The best neighbor is the one who can't be seen or heard or, as in my case, the one that doesn't even exist. I cannot imagine living in a place where I have to deal with a homeowners' or condo association, fools that write rules to please themselves. I would be a homeowners' association nightmare. I only cut my grass when I can't find my car, I play my Johnny Cash CDs as loud as I want and I throw my empty beer cans in the bush. When we get a good storm followed by a tidal surge the cans usually float out of the shrubbery and that's when I haul them off to the dumpster. My dogs are free to roam and poop where they please and I fly six flags along my beach. I display the flag of the Cayman Islands, the U.S., Scotland, Nova Scotia and one that illustrates a martini glass and olive. Scotland? Nova Scotia? Why, you may ask? Because I can.

Master Sgt. Denise James of Robinson Township, PA was sued by her condo association for flying an American flag in her yard between Memorial Day and the 4th of July. She is a member of the local Air National Guard. "This is a display for people serving currently, and people that have perished before us. It's just un-American that they don't want the flag being displayed," James said. The condo association is now suing her for $1,000 plus court costs and attorney fees. America – what a country! Stories like that that piss me off. On my planet, members of that homeowners' association would have been drafted and put on the front lines.

Then this lady in Oklahoma City, Oklahoma, purchased a new 32-foot Winnebago motor home. On a trip from an OU football game, she took the freeway. She set the cruise control at 70mph and calmly left the driver's seat to go to the back of the Winnebago to make herself a sandwich. Not surprisingly, the Winnebago left the highway and crashed. Not surprisingly, she sued Winnebago for not mentioning in the owner's manual that she couldn't actually leave the driver's seat while the cruise control was set. The Oklahoma jury awarded her... are you sitting down? A whopping $1.75 million plus a new motor home. Winnebago actually changed its manuals as a result of this suit. Shoot the members of that jury... I am on the wrong planet!

"One out of every four people on this planet is mentally unbalanced – think of your three closest friends... if they seem OK...Then you are the one."

TRAILER TRASH TV

I have a very bad habit of watching TV shows that piss me off and have me shouting obscenities at the TV screen. "X @*! Why are you people so f***ing stupid?"

Some medical folks call it the S.I. Syndrome, S.I. meaning self-injury. It's like being addicted to drugs... you know it's bad for you but you just can't stop. My mother once bought me the Jerry Springer DVD titled "Ringmaster". She's a Springer fan and would always say that I look like him. Well maybe, but knowing my mom I'm not sure if this was an insult or a compliment – she is a strange one; she belongs on this planet. The movie had a ridiculous plot; however I found it funny and entertaining.

I phoned her sometime later and she was most excited that I enjoyed the film.

"Well now, you gotta watch him on TV," she says. "He's on every day."

"No thanks mom. One Jerry Springer movie is enough for me."

"Not a movie son, the TV show is real."

"Mom, don't be naive... what I saw were actors in a movie playing the part of stupid Earthlings."

"On TV, son. On TV. It's not a movie... it's real."

I had to ignore her. After all, she also reads the *National Enquirer*. She called me the next day and insisted that I turn on my TV right then and there. "Now," she orders. "Go to channel 32. It's on right now."

I caved in... and couldn't believe what I was seeing. There it was – the TV version of the movie, but this was real. It was obvious these were not actors, just a bunch of idiots airing their dirty laundry. I am speechless watching Jerry's guests who volunteer their stupidity and ignorance to millions of viewers. There are more "bleeps" than words, they fight, they rip one another's clothes off and they reveal their wacky existence on this planet. Mothers sleeping with sons; sons sleeping with grandmothers; and prostitutes complaining their pimp is having an affair. Wow, this is rock-solid proof that I am on the wrong planet. On Planet Coherent the likes of Jerry Springer guests would be banished to Stuporous. I think Jerry Springer is from Coherent. I believe he is doing something good; he serves a purpose. He is paid a huge salary to remind us, the misplaced, that we are on the wrong planet.

The reality shows are another thorn in my butt. Yeah, right: I'm supposed to believe you are on a remote island, dehydrated and eating ants, when the 32 members of the film crew are gorging down a four-course lunch that was catered by a four-star hotel just around the bay. Pleeese... spare me the idiocy.

It takes very little to amuse little minds; however, I could be wrong with that quote. It's been said that the majority of reality show fans actually fall in the high IQ category. When I heard this all I could say was, "No way!" I can't believe that anyone with an IQ over 30 would believe that a crying scene on Big Brother hasn't been rehearsed and shot several times until the director gets just the right take. After all, if the director presents the network bosses a flawed or boring show, he can be replaced. So any ding-dong should concede that most of the unreal reality shows are simply edited, rehearsed, scripted plots to amuse the typical dim Earthling. Well, so I thought until one night I walked into my favorite pub. The joint was packed and noisy. "What's going on?" I thought. "It's not World Series or Super Bowl time... no heavyweight bouts that I know of." There on the big screen were the two remaining contestants of Survivor. Tonight, someone was going to win $1 million. I couldn't get to the bar; patrons were shoving, screaming, smoking and rooting for their favorite contender. They were a mix of lawyers, secretaries, doctors and bankers... I was taken aback. I ordered a cold brew in a plastic cup, walked down to the beach and sat alone staring at the heavens. Though I've never been there, I was missing Planet Coherent right about now... "Beam me up Scotty."

"Why pay to see garbage at a movie theater when you can see trash for free on TV?"

ADAPTORS

On Planet Coherent they have all the electronic gadgets as available on Planet Earth. Laptops, Nintendo, iPhones, smart phones, portable hand-held vacuum cleaners and the rest. One difference, however, considering those on Coherent are sound and consistent-thinking creatures, they keep things simple. The entire planet has the standard two forms of providing power – AC or DC. However, any portable appliance that receives the power has one simple adaptor that fits all. I have three beer boxes jammed with every adaptor, transformer or power supplier ever made. Each box is a tangled mishmash of wires and plugs indistinguishable from the snarled fish net in my boat. Some of the adaptors are for thingamajigs that haven't been manufactured for years. But I'm afraid to throw them away, because the moment I do – I'll need it. I have a collection of adaptors with 120 volt inputs and 45 mA along with 3.7 outputs, some have 50/60 Hz others with VDCs, 115 VAC and 15 Kw. What on Planet Earth does all that mean? Scanning the Internet for these confusing power supply adaptors is enough to give even Einstein a brain swell. Then there's the Universal Power supply kit that ought to work on any thingamabob. Ha! A big joke... if you don't have the right connector on your gadget, with the proper port and socket, you are screwed. "Why?" I ask. "Why keep it so complicated?" Some marketing people explain that by changing designs and models every few years it keeps the huge electronic companies in business. Fine, I have no problem with that... but why change the damn cord that supplies power to the latest model of my new portable hand drill? I recall an interview I once saw with one of the Beatles (John or Paul... forget which one). Anyway, he was asked what made their songs so appealing, so etched-in-your-mind popular? What's the secret ingredient for other aspirant song writers? "Just keep it simple," was the answer. On Planet Coherent all gadgets use the same adaptors – it's the law!

Some time back, I stopped at a super Best Buy store in Miami where I purchased a few DVDs – reruns of Green Acres (oh, I love that show). I noted on the box it said "Blu-ray Disc."

"Oh, no," I thought to myself. "Here we go again. Blue ray, green ray... I could care less. I just want to watch the show – so what is this?" I caught the attention of a clerk who looked very bored stocking the DVD racks.

"Excuse me sir, what's this Blu-ray thingy?"

"That's the latest thing out. Man, where have you been, on another planet?"

(Little did he know)

He went on to explain, "This Blu-ray DVD is so crystal clear it will make your eyes pop out. It has a blue violet laser which allows the picture to come through in greater precision. You'll think you're right there in the movie along with the actors."

Wow! To be in Green Acres and hang out with Mr. Haney and county agent Hank Kimball and my favorite character, Arnold the pig.

"I'll take it," I said. "In fact, I'll take the entire six seasons. Oh, I can't wait to climb the utility pole to use the phone."

The young sales clerk gave me an uncanny roll of the eyes and I knew what he was thinking: "Man, this guy is weird." A few evenings later, back in the Cayman Islands, 480 miles across the sea from the Best Buy store, I am preparing for my Green Acres marathon. Taco chips, onion dip, beef jerky and three 16-oz cans of ice-cold Foster's Australian beer. I Windex my spectacles and ease back in my easy chair... click the play button on the remote and – nothing! I click again... nothing! I get out of my easy chair and attempt to start my program manually... nothing. I check all the plugs, wires and put new batteries in my remote... and nothing! Damn that pisses me off! I call my gadget-and computer-savvy son.

"Hey Nick. I just bought $234 worth of DVDs, the Blu-ray kind. However, I can't get them to play... any suggestions?"

"Dad, did you also buy a Blu-ray player?"

"What's that?" I ask.

"Dad, you can't play Blu-ray DVDs on an old-fashioned DVD player."

"Old-fashioned... I bought this one at Wal-Mart just five years ago."

"Dad, that's old-fashioned... outdated."

"Why didn't they tell me that at the store?"

"Did you ask?"

"No!"

I call the Best Buy number as indicated on my receipt. I get a robot receptionist. You know, press one for this, and two for that. Time moves along and the call has come to an end with a busy signal. I call again... and again... and again...

Finally, 37 minutes after I first dialed the number, a human answers. I am so excited I can't speak for a second, and I'd misplaced my receipt number – I knew they would ask for it. "Hola... hola." "Speak English," I shout. "You are in America.".…."Hello, this is Best Buy. Hello... hello..." Click, they hang up... Damn that pisses me off !

I call the Best Buy corporate office in Richfield, Minnesota – it's like dealing with the CIA to get past the operators, secretaries and "whoever". Finally, doggedness won and I did get on line with a friendly, caring customer service person (who could speak English) and who held some executive position. Mr. Jones took time to listen to my complaint. He took down my email, phone number and address and three weeks later I had my Green Acres DVDs that worked in my outdated DVD player.

I like to give credit where credit is due – so I called the corporate office again to thank Mr. Jones for all his help.

"Glad to help," said Mr. Jones. "So sorry for all the troubles, not to mention all the overseas long distance calls you had to make. I'm sure that took up lots of your Green Acres time." I'm not sure if he was attempting to be sarcastic or simply keeping our conversation lighthearted.

"Well, Mr. Jones my long distance charges to Miami and your office cost me more than my Green Acres collection."

"What... why don't you use a Vonage phone?" he says.

"A what?"

"Vonage... Vonage... you can make overseas calls using high-speed broadband Internet, and call anywhere, for about $10 per month."

"Wow that sounds interesting. Is that the latest electronic gadget on the market?"

"Sir, it's been around for years. What planet have you been on?"

"I'm an old dinosaur, Mr. Jones. Where would I get one of these gizmos?"

"You know what, Mr. Nowak? For all the frustrations and extra costs to get your DVDs, Best Buy will ship you a Vonage phone as a gift."

"Are you serious? Wow, thank-you so much... does it come with an adaptor?"

"Yes, of course, and all you need to do is remove the Ethernet cable from the modem, then insert it into the Ethernet port on the Vonage phone device. You can also use a separate Ethernet cable which may be necessary if you do not use a wireless router, or if you care..."

"Mr. Jones, Mr. Jones! Stop... stop... thanks, but no thanks."

LET'S EAT

I can't believe all the fat people on this planet – especially in America, land of plenty. Plenty Burger Kings, Wendy's, McDonald's, etc. It's been said if you could convert back to food all that excess calorie intake of the obese people in America, you could feed all the starving in Africa. It's been said? Then again, all the money that so many African nations spend on weapons and camouflage uniforms could also be spent to feed their poor. Let's not go there, that subject pisses me off.

When I say fat I am not talking about chunky, beer-belly or even overweight couch potatoes. I'm talking about bodies that put sumo wrestlers to shame. Monster flab overload where one can hide a slice of pizza between the layers of flesh. Hey, I'm no muscle-toned "hunk"; my brew consumption is evident around my waistline. Then there's my craving for conch fritters deep-fried in cooking oil and fresh lobster tails smothered in lemon butter.... Mmmmmm!

But junk food for breakfast, lunch and dinner... day after day after day... what is wrong with some of these Earthlings? On Planet Coherent, the floor tiles in front of every cashier in a McDonald's, Burger

King or KFC is actually a scale. This feature is a must – it's the law. Before the counter clerk takes your order your weight is automatically entered into the cash register. If you are more than 50 pounds over your average body weight the register locks up and the clerk cannot take your order. In other words, you don't get your fries, double cheese Whopper and the paper hat. Don't attempt to fool them at the drive-through window because on Coherent there is no such a thing. If you're in the weight perimeter to eat junk food every day, then at least get out of your car and get some exercise by walking inside. On Coherent, all fast food eateries have their parking areas two blocks away – it's the law. If you attempt to park in the no-parking area near the restaurant you will be severely punished. You will be locked up for two weeks and fed only salads and water. Oh, don't you just love my planet?

On Planet Coherent all businesses must promote good health – it's the law. On Coherent obese people don't get lunch breaks. It's simple: no food, no calories. However, if you choose, you can take your lunch break at the gym.

Go ahead... throw the book at me (this book). Go ahead... scream discrimination, inequality, unjust. Sorry, Earthlings. On my planet if you take up two seats on an airplane (one for body and one for flab) you pay for two seats. If you don't like it... you walk – and walking from Miami to New York will burn calories. I've had the displeasure of being assigned a window seat next to a walrus and a terrorist. The terrorist being the eight-year-old spoiled-brat son of the walrus – both should have their jaws fused. The little terrorist would jump up and down in his seat, throw spit-balls and spill his sugar-loaded soft drink in my lap – all while the walrus snored louder than the sound of the jet engines. After a few double shots of Bacardi to calm my nerves I needed to go to the loo. I was doing my best to refrain from using the restroom, so when my kidneys were about to burst I asked to be excused.

The walrus began to huff and puff as he attempted to pull his wedged blubber from the aisle seat. The terrorist was squeezing his groin shouting, "Me too... me too... I gotta go to the bathroom." The father heaved a sigh and said, "Sir, since you are going that way, would you take him for me?" I walk the kid back to the back of the plane, place him in a vacant bathroom and remind him to wash his hands before he comes out – I don't want pissy paws in the seat beside me.

"But I can't get my pee-pee out. You gotta help me – my daddy always helps me."

"No way," I said "I'm not touching your pee-pee kid – you can piss in your pants for all I care."

I can just see it now – the little monster telling everyone I pulled his pants down and touched his pee-pee and the US Air Marshall puts me in handcuffs then drags me off the plane upon landing. Just imagine later that night, Nancy Dis-Grace flashes my picture all over CNN.

"No way kid, you get in there and do the best you can."

The kid starts to scream: "It hurts – it hurts!" Every passenger turns back to see me holding the bathroom door open. Then he pisses his pants. I knew I should have taken the Greyhound!

Why is it that I have to pay for extra luggage – yet an obese person with excess baggage does not? They make a law that says I can't smoke my cigar in a public place because the second-hand smoke is unhealthy for those around me – yet those around me clog up their arteries at junk food establishments that specialize in grease, sugar and salt. In my opinion, some Earthlings abuse their children: they feed their offspring what their offspring wants to eat – pizza, candy and super-gulp sodas. Then, if that isn't enough, they stick a remote control in their hands so the kid can become champion at some violent video game instead of victor at some outdoor sport. No matter, if you are fat or skinny, if you're a parent, it's your responsibility to feed your litter something green now and then. Call me cold-hearted and condemn me for my utter lack of sensitivity, however, I actually do feel sorry for the fat little butterballs who waddle down the grocery aisle as colossal mama fills a shopping cart with ice cream and chips completely avoiding the fruit and vegetable counters.

In my childhood days I can't recall too many of my friends being fat or obese – we played outside till sunset. We had no PlayStations, Nintendos or Xboxes. There were no video games, no 150 channels on cable, no DVDs, no surround-sound or CDs, no cell phones, no personal computers, no Internet and no chat rooms. We hung out, we moved, we ran, we swam, climbed trees and we fought – we had friends and we had to go outside to find them.

On Planet Coherent obese people pay higher taxes than others. Prejudice you say? Not so. Why should the taxpayer who makes an attempt to stay reasonably healthy pay for the unnecessary medical cost of obese people? Diseases associated with excess weight such as heart attacks, diabetes and osteoarthritis are overloading Planet Earth with $147 billion dollars in medical bills accumulated annually in America alone. And maybe there are some whose eating habits are due to a medical condition – maybe. However, I just don't buy the excuse that most who eat a barrel of KFC or three Big Macs do it because they have a gland problem. It's possible that obese people are part of the global warming effect. They certainly need more clothes to cover up their huge bodies, which mean more raw materials are used. They eat more, so they produce more greenhouse gases. They consume more fuel because it costs less to transport thin people. Fat people drive more because they can't walk to the corner convenience store so they need bigger cars, which burn more gas.

On Planet Coherent we have obese people – after all, no place is perfect. However, our numbers are not even close to a place called America on Planet Earth, where almost 20 million people are 60 pounds too heavy. In other words: 1 billion, 200 million pounds of fat. With that surplus of blubber, we could save the whales when Planet Earth has run out of crude oil, when we have to go back to whale oil lamps. It is of my opinion the judicial system has something to do with the obese problem.

True story: big fat 300-and-something-pound *Malia Lundan had an argument with her boyfriend *Mickey Middle. Later, while Mickey was snoozing on the couch, Malia sat on his face and smothered him to death. That's a horrible way to die. I'd rather be blindfolded and shot by a firing squad or eaten by a great white shark than have some huge, disgusting-smelling booty squashing my nose – if you attempt to inhale... Yuggg. If you attempt to exhale – you can't. I'm feeling faint just writing this. She was charged with involuntary manslaughter. Manslaughter? What about man-smother and why involuntary? Ya, right! Poor old Mickey was flapping around like an octopus and she just kept on eating her fried chicken while watching Jerry Springer. You couldn't hear Mickey because her big, fat flabby ass was plastered across his head. She couldn't see the quiver of Mickey's arms or legs because she had no view beyond the rolls of flab around her waistline. Now we're supposed to believe that it was an accident? The judge obviously bought her story because she sentenced her to three years probation and 100 hours of community service. Now let's scrutinize that sentence – 100 hours of community service. If you put in eight hours per day that would mean in less than two weeks she's done her time for performing one of the most sickening, gruesome murders imaginable. And what will her community service require? Sweeping the street, teaching homeless children to play volleyball, painting the church and, of course, she's allowed to have lunch and coffee breaks. How dim-witted. What was that judge thinking? Malia can't even move 10 feet without sitting down to catch her breath. As for the three years probation – it means nothing, only words. What the judge did do, however, is set a precedent. In other words, you don't need to hire a hit man if you want to eliminate your cheating, lazy, unemployed partner. Just go to Cleveland, Ohio, and smother your troublesome spouse with a pillow. Then, when the cops show up, sit on his face, cry a little and say you're sorry... 100 hours of community service later, you are free. Ahh... America, what a country! Then again, maybe I shouldn't judge the judge. Maybe she was wiser than I'll ever be. Maybe she had one look at the defendant and thought: "The state is on a tight budget. We could never afford to feed Ms. Malia. Plus, the state would have to build a special oversized holding pen... the average cell could never hold her. How would we transport her to and from prison?" Maybe the 100 hours was a good thing.

* Malia and Mickey's names have been changed – but the incident did happen.

"I found there is only one way to look thin – hang out with fat people."
– Rodney Dangerfield

100 percent guaranteed way to lose weight... stop eating

STOP AND SMELL THE FLOWERS

My very close friend and band mate Chuck is in a rush. He's always in a rush. He sprints through an airport terminal while we tag along 10 feet behind. In a relaxed gathering with friends he will finish his food and drink, and pop up like a jack-in-the-box and shout: "OK – it's time to go!" I don't pay him much attention – he's just on the wrong island, like I'm on the wrong planet. Chuck is from Long Island, New York, population around eight million and he has been misplaced on a relaxed tropical island of 55,000. As a touring band, we may travel by road or sea. Whatever our means of travel, Chuck needs to be behind the wheel to make sure he can get from point A to point B as quick as possible. I consider myself a very laid-back, untroubled individual; however, around my friend Chuck, his stress wears off on me and I start popping blood pressure pills – rush, rush, rush. I am amazed how he can keep his life and business in order when moving and thinking at such a fast pace. Slow down Earthlings – stop and smell the flowers.

Joshua Bell, one of the greatest musicians on Planet Earth, opened his violin case and began to play the instrument, valued at $3.5 million, in a

Washington, DC metro station. Mr. Bell normally plays in theaters that sell seats for $100. Today, however, he is part of a social experiment about people's priorities. He left his violin case open at his feet and the Grammy award-winning violinist started to play, performing several classical pieces in a 45-minute incognito concert. Over 1,000 people passed by him and only seven took time to stop, look and listen. He collected a total of $32.00 and change in tips. This true story blows me away. Not that I am some big classical music buff, but how can 1,000 people choose their office desk and computers over beautiful music? Rush, rush, rush... Where are your priorities Earthlings? It's only money, it's only stress – maybe a possible promotion, and for that you missed a free 45-minute concert by a master playing on a handcrafted 1713 Stradivarius. I can deal with my good friend Chuck but there are some "rushers" that I despise: those that beep at you to move the split second a traffic light turns green. Man that pisses me off!

Once I got so infuriated that I placed my vehicle in park, got out of my car and walked back to the impatient "beeper".

With a (I'd-like-to-shoot-you) sarcastic smile I say, "Yes... can I help you?"

"Well, the light had turned green and you were not moving," says the very annoyed taxi driver.

"Oh, I'm sorry. I thought you had just wanted to chat," I respond.

"No, I want you to move."

As I'm being a smartass, the cars start to line up and now everyone starts beeping.

"Sir, do you realize it takes the average brain one-third of a second to register the color change of an average traffic light?"

"No, I never thought of that," said the cabbie.

"Well sir, you started beeping at me one-quarter of a second before my brain had a chance to record that the light had turned green, so when you beeped I had not yet registered that it was time to go. Now, considering that my brain has dealt with many hangovers in my 60 years on a planet that I'm not supposed to be on, it is possible that it could take almost a full second for my brain to register the green light."

The taxi driver seemed dumfounded at my boldness, yet impressed with my knowledge of how the brain functions at a traffic light. All he could say: "Gee, I never thought of that."

"Well sir, I just fabricated this traffic light mumbo-jumbo to kill time... now please consider by the time I walk back to my car the light will have turned red again, and then we have to wait for the green light... so please don't beep for at least one second once the traffic light changes."

As I walked back to my vehicle, the cabbie craned his head out of the window; he just had to get in the last word. "What planet are you from?" I smile at my reflection in the rearview mirror... "Oh, that felt good."

What are your priorities? What if someone told you had only one year to live, what would you do? Would you rush-rush to get all the things done on your bucket list? Well, no one wants to be faced with morbid news; however, it could be a blessing. If I had a confirmed date on my mortality I would spend my nest egg, the savings I have been setting aside for a rainy day. I would smoke five Cuban cigars a day instead of saving my Montecristo Reserves for special occasions. I'd drink more beer and eat more pizza. I'd accept the invitations to cocktail parties and, while there, I'd irritate everyone with belches and farts. I'd do a lot of fishing because there is no such thing as a bad day out at sea with a hand line in one hand and a beer in the other. But if my last 12 months on Earth left me with one final wish, I'd wish to live it out on a deserted, tropical island surrounded by warm seas and blue skies. An island full of pigs would be fine. But please, no humans. When my 365 days are up and I'm six feet under – please come by and visit. Take time to stop and smell the flowers, the flowers on my grave, which will be plastic, fake and artificial, like so many of the humans in this sphere. Life can be tough for a misplaced heretic on the wrong planet. Subscription television service channel Showtime has a hit. Dexter proves that I can't be all wrong – he eliminates child molesters and drug dealers... and has won Golden Globe awards doing so.

CHILD CRUELTY "PUNISHMENT"

When I was in elementary and junior high school it was an era of simplicity: no bottled water, no safety bike helmets and no seatbelts. Somehow, along with millions of others now past the age of 50, we survived. The only belt I ever got was off my stepfather's jeans when I did something impish. He would pull off his belt, double it up and say: "I'm going to wop your ass... one day this week." Then, he'd send me to bed. Now that was torture, mental cruelty, because I never knew when I was going to get it. I'd walk around on eggshells day after day avoiding my stepfather whenever I could. I'd take out the trash and wash the dishes and eat all my spinach. And then with no forewarning, while I'm watching "Lassie" on the black-and-white TV, came the volatile leather strap across my legs or ass... my mother would come running in and put a stop to it and, again, I'm sent to bed, but relieved it was finally all over. I'd fall asleep plotting ways to slay my stepfather – I could throw gas on him while he's passed out drunk and set him on fire. Then again, my poor mom, brothers and sister would be sleeping in the streets and I would be locked up in some reform school. I could shoot him – however my mother had already thrown his pistol in a nearby lake some time ago.

If any parent used this "leather strap" form of punishment nowadays, the minor could climb out the back window, flag down the sheriff and have the parents thrown in jail for child abuse. The minor could find a lawyer at legal aid and sue the parents for everything they got... which, in most cases, is nothing.

"Thou shalt beat him with the rod, and deliver his soul from hell." Proverbs 23:13-14. Yes, I know what you're thinking – why am I quoting the Bible? Hypocrite. Hey, it's a good quote, it makes sense and that's also the rule of thumb on Planet Coherent. Look at this Planet Earth – a place filled with laxity and tolerance. Children control the parents, and by the time they reach college age the parents deport them to a university with a new car, credit cards and a fake ID. In no time, the spoiled dependents are throwing up at frat parties and skipping class. Well mommy, daddy, that's what you get when you use "time-out" instead of a good whack across the head. To spank or not to spank – that is the question. Spare the rod, raise a delinquent.

On Coherent spanking is encouraged so punks are few. As much as I wanted to exterminate my stepfather at the time, I now appreciate his floggings and military-style rearing. I know this sounds trite but I honestly believe it has made me a better person. In our household it was a matter of rule to say "please", "thank-you", "yes ma'am", "yes sir". I wouldn't even consider talking back to parents – in fact, to any adult. If I did... I'd be DEAD MEAT. And had I ever kicked or even pinched my mom in a tantrum, I'd not be writing this book... the worms would have disposed of me decades ago. I get infuriated when I see some bratty juvenile having a temper outburst in a restaurant or supermarket. They scream, kick, bite and scratch while mommy and daddy take the punishment. I wanna just take a saturated Pamper and whack the un-mindful parents across the head. You can't blame the brat; his parents made him that way and once that kid reaches the age of nine or 10, it's too late – all goes downhill. And then those same kids grow up and become parents... OMG – I hope I'm six feet under by then.

Another lesson I learned from my stepfather (who was a real redneck) was that the stick is mightier than the fist. As a very young lad we lived in a small village in Germany. I recall one day my mother had sent me down to the butcher shop to pick up some sausages. I didn't want to go – there were a few bullies down the road that always picked on me. They'd throw rocks and call me offensive anti-American names. My mother had re-married to a military man in the USAF and because of my ties with my American stepfather I was continually harassed by the local German kids. They were not big fans of anyone connected with the U.S. military, the invaders that defeated them in WWII just a decade earlier. I figure I was about eight or nine years old when I came home that day in tears and a handful of dirty, squashed bratwurst. I explained to my stepfather what had happened – the local bullies struck again. He took me by the hand and we walked towards the village. On the way he broke a sturdy limb off a pine tree.

"Ha, I thought – now those little Nazi bastards will get their due."

"Show me where this happened," he demanded.

I identified the spot and saw the bullies. "There they go papa... see them... that's them running through the bush."

Instead of running after them, he threw the stick in the bushes along the path. "You're not gonna go after them papa? Why did you throw the stick away?"

"No, I'm not going after them and I am leaving that stick there for you. The next time the little Hitlers start picking on you, I want you to take that stick and beat the German crap out of them."

"Huh," is all I could say.

"You heard me, forget a fist fight – fight dirty. You have the right. You are one and there are three of them. Just pick up that stick, chase them down, and beat 'em."

"But... but..." I started to cry.

"No buts. If you don't, I'll come back and get the stick and beat the crap out of you."

I was confused and upset that my mom accepted my stepfather's ruling. Maybe she was scared of him or maybe she felt that I needed a strong father figure to make me a tough lad (like the boy named Sue). Whatever, I dreaded the day I'd again be sent on a mission to the butcher shop. When that day finally came the oppressors were waiting for me, but not for long – I followed my stepfather's orders and swung that stick, striking anything within my reach. One of the tormenters took off after I made contact with his left eye and the other was in the dirt begging for mercy. I was swinging, swearing and sweating out of control – but it felt good. The butcher came out of his shop, took my stick and sent me home sausage-less. I wasn't unscratched, the bloody nose and dirt between my teeth was evidence of a battle. My mom wailed as she cleaned me off and my stepfather passed me a beer. He further rewarded me with a rare pat on the head and a few compliments. The next day my mother bought me a pet rabbit – she figured I needed a friend since I was now Public Enemy No. 1 in our village. I loved that little white bunny. One day when I returned home from school he was gone – he had wiggled his way out of the flimsy cage I had constructed. I rummaged through every crack, cranny and bush looking for "Fuzzy", my cute little bunny and friend. And then I got the shocking news. He had escaped into the neighbor's yard and... she ate him! That night I sniveled myself to sleep and planned revenge. I wanted the old hare-eating witch to die. Sadly, she never did. However the local bullies stayed clear of me.

But you ought to thank me, before I die,
For the gravel in your guts
and the spit in your eye,
Cause I'm the son-of-a-bitch
that named you "Sue".
– From Johnny Cash's "Boy Named Sue"

STUPID PEOPLE – STUPID MOVIES AND GAMES

Yes, we have a small population of stupid people on Planet Coherent; can't escape stupidity. There are stupid people everywhere – Coherent is no exception. What's amazing is that even smart, educated people can be stupid, so this goes back to something I've said before; when I say stupid I am not talking about a lack of education or lack of a college diploma, or being unhealthy with some mental disorder. I'm talking plain stupid. On Planet Earth so many young kids are influenced by TV, movies, music and video games. Hollywood actually creates, develops and promotes stupidity. Hollywood has kids thinking that packing a pistol is trendy, that the shoot 'em up scenes are real. Thanks to TV these kids think the swearing, pimping, drug dealing and calling girls "bitches" will make them a big hero. So, after they turn off the TV, they go out in the world to copy their TV or movie idols. They are too dumb to realize that their idols are often performers getting paid to act cool and stupid. In the real world, the bullets are real and the getaway car that speeds through the crowded streets is a deadly weapon.

Long ago I saw a TV news report where they were producing a story on what influence TV and video games have on young children. The segment that really got my attention was an interview with a kindergarten teacher. She had asked her class to match letters of the alphabet with words. In other words A is for apple, B is for bird and so on. One five-year-old in the class matched B with bitch and K with AK-47. Doesn't that just make you wanna whack some parents across the head?

Planet Coherent has resolved this absurdity – well not 100 percent – but it is way ahead of Planet Earth. It's a simple technique and Coherents can't figure out why some dumb Earthling hasn't thought of it. Just like the FBI warning at the start of a video that reminds viewers not to duplicate, on Coherent all movies, video games and music in the violent, crude, rape, foul-mouth category start with a warning. The warning is verbal and in text on the screen. It reads, and is spoken slowly by a narrator – and the narrator giving the warning is also the bad guy in the movie. "Warning: what you are about to see or hear is not true – these are actors or out-of-tune rappers". Half way through the movie or video game, just as the carnage gets real intense, the movie or video game is interrupted when another visual and narrated alert pops up on the screen: "Warning: if you think what you're watching is real you are a dim-witted fool." At the end of the movie, just before the credits roll, one final message is spoken very loudly: "Warning: what you just saw was fake. You saw actors in a make-believe movie (or animated characters in a make-believe video game). If you leave this theater thinking it was real you are a mindless idiot."

Now, this may sound a bit harsh, but even stupid people don't want to be called stupid so they leave the theater programmed not to be stupid. As for educational-style documentaries with brutal subject matter – the warnings are not necessary. After all, stupid people don't watch documentaries. Stupid parents, however, let their kids watch violent video games. Some parents even purchase these games as a birthday or Christmas gift. Games that include blood splatter, innocent people being run over by speeding automobiles, crude language and gore. While some judges support a law that would make the sale of such video games to minors illegal, others are raising concerns about free speech. Free speech is the freedom to speak your mind. Just what does this have to do with prohibiting minors from watching an animated rape scene? One thing is for sure: violence in video games sells and for a long time the younger generation has been bored with Pac-Man eating dots.

There is a Japanese marketed video game called "RapeLay"... it actually simulates rape. The game is played from the perspective of a chikan named Kimura Masaya, who stalks and subsequently rapes the Kiryuu family (a mother and her two young daughters). The player can choose from a variety of sexual positions, and controls the action by making movements with the mouse or by scrolling the mouse wheel. It features a realistic sexual simulator, which allows the player to grope and undress the characters on a crowded train. Later, the player may have forced intercourse with all three women at his leisure. The player has a variety of sexual positions to choose from such as reverse cowgirl, forced blow jobs (irrumatio), and threesomes. RapeLay also has a "nakadashi" (internal ejaculation) counter, which carries a danger of pregnancy. How would we handle the distribution of this game on my planet? We simply drop another bomb on Japan.

THE PETER PAN SYNDROME

The Peter Pan Syndrome is a very common condition on Coherent. In fact it's a sure sign that you are in the company of a true Coherent if you notice their Peter Pan Syndrome. One of my ex-wives once told me I had the Peter Pan Syndrome. Not knowing what she meant I Googled – Peter Pan Syndrome. Here is what I got: Peter Pan is a fictional character created by author J. M. Barrie in the early 1900s. He is a boy who never wants to grow up, flying off to Never-Never Land and embarking on a variety of adventures. Mmmmm. OK, she is right so far. It goes on to say some individuals mature into adulthood physically, but have difficulty in social situations – Mmmmm, right again. The description continues: The idea that some people refuse to grow up is hardly new. People with Peter Pan Syndrome suffer in social situations because they are unable to process adult issues. Yep... right again. Because Peter Pan Syndrome is not a recognized psychological issue, there is no established treatment. As with many psychological issues, treatment is most effective when the patient actively seeks it out and wants to modify his or her behavior, as this will mean that the patient is willing to put in the work to make the treatment work.

What a crock of B.S. So effin' what?! Let me scrutinize this "Peter Pan Syndrome." Yes, I have difficulty in social situations. And, yes, I admit, I suffer when attending some gathering beyond the boundaries of my local pub. I hate snob-nosed cocktail parties or company award ceremonies... they are so phony.

"Hello, Mrs. Jones. You look lovely today." Yet I'm actually thinking: "Here comes that disgusting bad-breath Jonsey whose fat-ass husband is the biggest kiss-ass on the island."

Oh no – she wants me to kiss her on the cheek – and then the other cheek... "BARF."

"Oh, and that's my angel Tommy," she says, pointing towards her five-year-old. "He's grown into such a handsome lad and so full of energy."

And I'm thinking: "I wish that little snotty nosed brat would stop running around – he's really getting on my nerves. Hope he chokes on that hot dog."

I know what you're thinking right now: "Why am I there in the first place?" Well as an entertainer and musician I have had to play my share of weddings, corporate conventions and once even for Prince Charles at a royal ball. Not my favorite "gigs" but I have bills to pay like anyone else. I must have a bad case of this Peter Pan Syndrome – flying off to Never-Never Land and embarking on a variety of adventures. Now, what's the problem with that? My refusal to grow up and act like most so-called responsible Earthlings has taken me on a variety of adventures. I have traveled to Ireland and stayed in castles. I've cruised through the canals of Venice in a gondola. I've sailed on yachts through the South Seas from Samoa to Tahiti to Bora Bora to Hawaii. I've gone pearl diving in Manihiki and drank schnapps in the Alps of Switzerland. I've smoked the best cigars in Cuba and I've been locked up in prison in Nassau, Bahamas. Never a boring moment... except when I'm at a social gathering around grown-ups who are not lucky enough to have the Peter Pan Syndrome. It's tough living on a planet where one is scorned upon for not acting their age or criticized for wanting to fly to Never- Never Land. I guess my ex-wife was right.

I have had a recurring dream for many years. In my dream I am high on a rocky bluff and in the distance across the sea there is a tropical island encircled with a barrier reef. I can see white sandy beaches and swaying palms. With my arms extended like the wings of a booby bird, I run to the edge of the bluff and take off. To the amazement of my friends watching below, I make my way towards the island. I can see half-naked, alluring brown-skinned girls below coaxing me to land. Every time I attempt to land a gust of wind pulls me up again. I make another attempt; however the air-currents are too strong. I make my way back to the bluff where there are no trade winds and the terrain is barren. One day I will land, and when I do I'll never wake up again – I'll be dead – with an erection and a smile.

RAPPERS

I can digest just about any style of music, be it classical, country, reggae, soul or rock. However I simply can't swallow hip-hop, Jamaican Dance Hall, opera and bag pipes. Yet my biggest turn off is rap: I just don't get it. The boom-boom of the unsettling bass intermingled with anti-everything-you-can-imagine lyrics: "slap the bitch"... " kill the pigs"... "bring back my mother-f'in' money and my mother-f'in' dope", etc. I just don't get it! Now, having said that, I will also say: "Each to his own." If that turns you on, then turn up the volume. Even on Coherent, the freedom of musical tastes is like freedom of speech – if your ears and brain can adapt... turn up the volume higher

Let's forget the lyrics and so-called music for a moment. What really perplexes me about rap is: why don't rappers smile? Why do they look so mean and ready to kill? There's no reason for the grimace; these guys should be grinning ear-to-ear. Jay-Z, for example, made over $63 million between 2009 and 2010. These guys fly around in Lear jets, adorn themselves with gold chains and gold-filled teeth, stay at five-star hotels along with their massive entourage and live in 10-bathroom houses – and yet they're always pissed off. I don't get it. This is not a color issue or a racist synopsis. Look at Eminem: he's whiter than I am, and I've never seen a picture of him with a smile on his face. Oh well, maybe he has an excuse – he only makes around $12 million a year.

When I receive my off-and-on royalty checks from BMI or iTunes downloads I am happy as a dog with two tails. My last huge royalty deposit amounted to just over $1,900 and I was ecstatic. Should I receive a meager $1 million, it's very possible that my jawbone would crack from the immense grin on my face. So why are rappers so unappreciative? The look is a serious look for the most part; rap and hip-hop record execs believe the scarier you look, the better you sell. Oh, now I get it... that's what I'm doing wrong! That's why I get skimpy royalty payments. OK, on my next album cover I'm going to have a picture of myself in a Freddy Krueger costume and give myself a new name like "Toe-cheese", or something stupid like that. Hey, why not? That's another part of the success story – you need a strange stage name like Beenie Man, Puff Daddy, Snoop Dogg or Psycho Les. And what about Curtis James Jackson III, who calls himself 50 Cent? Just think of the irony of that rapper's name. The guy has made about $90 million and he calls himself 50 Cent? Man, I'm I on the wrong planet!

And what's with the grabbing-their-crotch thing? I'm not even going to go there. Am I jealous? You're damn right I am, not about the size of their "joystick" but about all the money they make. I've made my living as a musician and songwriter for over 35 years. I've smiled on my album covers, I've composed happy songs about sun, sand and sea, I have no gold in my teeth or pistol in my back pocket and I have never worn a baseball cap sideways or in reverse. So, for all those well-mannered, gracious and grinful years I get a lousy $1,900 royalty check. Forget what I said earlier about being ecstatic over my royalty check... I'm pissed off, so I just wrote a rap song.

"Hey all you damn rappers,
You better look out,
I just bought a gold chain
and put gold in my mouth,
If ya get in my way
I'm gonna have to kill ya.
And if you don't die
I'm gonna have to bill ya
And I'll steal all you money
from your till-a,
And if ya bend over baby
I'm gonna have to drill ya,
And if I were a fish I would have to gill ya
And baby you're so hot
I'm gonna have to grill ya
And this song is as boring
as a sleepin' pill ya..."

There is no law against rap music on Coherent; it's just that on my planet anyone making $90 million is a very happy soul. Oh, one more thing... what's with keeping the price tag on your baseball cap? I can't imagine how that could be considered cool when it looks so stupid. Why not keep your dental bill attached to your gold tooth? Though I have never attended a rap concert I have accidently had a sneak peek while changing channels with my remote. I notice the camera panning through the thousands of happy fans in the audience. There are blacks, whites, Orientals and grandmas, all swaying to the tuneless, often detestable lyrics. The rappers grab their crotch and perform strange movements with their hands and make millions of dollars doing it – "Beam me up Scotty!"

"Anything that is too stupid to be spoken... is sung."
– Voltaire

HOMELESS PEOPLE

I'm sorry, I just don't buy it. Unless you have some sort of handicap, or are in a wheelchair, too old to move and have no family, there is no excuse for being homeless and leeching off the kindness of others to get your bottle of cheap wine. It pisses me off when I'm at a stoplight and some smelly creep holds up a sign reading – "Please help me I'm a veteran, need food." Bullshit... I note you have two legs, two hands and a flask of whiskey in your pocket... go get a job! If you are truly a veteran you can still find a job, probably quicker than a draft dodger. If you were truly hurt in a war and that has resulted in some sort of handicap, well... thank-you for fighting for our freedom. Seriously, I mean that. Isn't the government then obligated to take care of you? They should anyway. However, for you others, those of you impersonating a veteran, work is there if you really want it. Take Miami as an example: nearly every other cab driver is from Haiti. Some of these guys washed up on shore with nothing except the drenched clothes on their back and within six months they have a job. I've been to Haiti: what a disgusting place. You can't blame these poor folks for swimming through shark-infested waters in hopes for any type of employment. Am I making my point here? If immigrant Haitians can do it – why not you lazy bums? Those who feel sorry for the homeless will argue that most have mental problems or schizophrenia or manic depression. I believe that – what do you expect when you mix cheap alcohol and heroin with lazy? In Los Angeles there are some 12,000 homeless living on Skid Row, yet farmers have to hire illegal migrants to pick apples because the healthy homeless citizens would rather beg than work. It simply doesn't add up.

The American Civil Liberties Union (ACLU) will say: "But it's their prerogative if they choose to be lazy. Leave them alone." OK, I agree with that – but why should they be allowed to piss in the streets and block an intersection and demand that taxpayers feed them and pay for their booze? Makes no sense... Damn, I'm on the wrong planet.

Actor Gene Hackman whacked some bum in the mouth for making a derogatory remark towards his wife. Of course the press was too spineless to call the bum a bum so the headlines read: "Gene Hackman Strikes Homeless Man". Dear Editor: what does it matter if the guy was homeless? A creep is a creep. Good job, Gene.

On Coherent there are few homeless, and those few will be picked up on a worldwide, bi-annual planet spring cleaning. While in a temporary holding pen they are fed, clothed and receive a full physical exam. Those healthy enough to work will be sent out to sweep streets, clean public toilets and dig ditches, saving the taxpayers millions of dollars. For a few months they will be allowed free housing and meals with NO BOOZE! Government will eventually find them a paying job and they are expected to keep it. Catch you back begging and boozing, it's off to Stuporous with you! Stuporous makes Haiti look like paradise. There were an estimated 11.6 million unauthorized immigrants living in the United States as of January 2008. An estimated 6.6 million of the 11.6 million unauthorized residents were from Mexico. Most of these illegals quickly find work in the Land of Opportunity. Jobs are there: so why are there 12,000 of you lazy asses in Los Angeles begging on the street corner? Let's get something cleared up. I am simply trying to make a point – there is work if you want it. I do not support illegal immigrants. I say deport them and let's deduct $100,000 per illegal from the foreign aid America annually donates to Mexico, which, by the way, exceeds $30 million.

Freedom is a good thing – that's why I love America so much. Sure, the country has its shortcomings but freedom is another motivation why so many jump over the razor wire fences. Why aren't these illegals sneaking into Jamaica, San Salvador or Somalia? Sure, many cross the border for jobs at Wal-Mart, for a better way of life, but the true objective is freedom. If you give the middle finger to an authoritarian in China or Iran, you could end up on the wrong end of a firing squad. However, in America the same gesture is called "freedom of speech." I am of the opinion that freedom can go too far. In other words, let's compare freedom to a bottle of aspirin. If you take a few as prescribed it can be a wonder drug. If you take the whole bottle... it can kill you. Let's take neo-Nazis (again): they are the epitome of a**holes. They hate everyone except Hitler. Just think about it: they worship a monster who gassed millions, a dictator who experimented on children and ordered the systematic murder of the disabled. Yet in America neo-Nazis can freely raise their hand and publicize their "Seig Heil!" Now that's freedom out of control and that pisses me off. Fortunately for the neo-Nazis, they are on the right planet. Should any of them show their swastikas on Planet Coherent their freedom of speech would come to an abrupt end. I hate neo-Nazis!

Freedom... freedom... Take MTV, a station that used to air some of the best musical videos – everything from old Beatles black-and-white clips to Michael Jackson's classic "Thriller". Now it's become a channel of monotonous sexism, tight jeans and a view of every pierced body part that the FCC (Federal Communications Commission) will allow to be shown. What really pisses me off is that I've caught my kids watching it. When they would, I'd put on a George Jones CD and turn the volume way up – that's all it would take for the remote click to shut down the tube. Then there's stations with their unreal reality shows like Sex Rehab – damn, what is this world coming to? Sex Rehab documents the treatment of sexual addiction. What on Planet Earth does sexual addiction mean? What is wrong with being addicted to sex? Then there's BET Network, nothing wrong with that, but where is

WET Network (White Entertainment Television)? OMG, Al Sharpton would give birth to a white baby.

Sitting in Durty Reids Bar I once asked the "BET – WET" question to close friend of mine (who is very black). He had an interesting response – "I don't care much for BET except for those huge jelly-shaking booties in the musical videos. But, keep in mind, BET employs a lot of colored folks."

"Well, so do drug dealers," I said. We both stared in our beer glass for a second and changed the subject. He wasn't mad at my sarcasm. We just couldn't figure out what that conversation accomplished.

Clearly the 9-11 terrorist attacks have taken a big toll on freedom. I've heard many bitch and moan about the hassles of TSA airport security. The X-rays, the puffer machines, the body scanners, the removal of belts, shoes and coins.

"They're infringing on my civil rights," some whine. "I have a right to privacy!" shout others. "It's a waste of time, I could miss my flight."

Well, what if there were two lines at New York's JFK airport. Each line leads to a different EL AL (National flag carrier of Israel) aircraft. Both planes are going to the same destination, Tel Aviv, Israel. One departure line has the usual TSA X-ray checks, scanners and passport checks. The other departure line is just a simple walk down the boarding bridge and onto your plane without any questions asked. Which line would you take? Go ahead: take some of my freedom away... I want to arrive at my destination. Four in 10 people say the U.S. government should have greater power to monitor the activities of suspicious, possible terrorist living in the United States. Four out of 10? Why aren't 10 out of 10 in agreement to monitoring anyone suspicious? I must be on the wrong planet – how could anyone see scrutinizing potential terrorists, neo-Nazis or child molesters as the removal of their freedom? They are lucky to be free.

"OK lady, before you board this plane take off that burka. Let's see if you have an AK-47 or a box cutter on you."

"But you can't make me do that Mr. TSA-man. You are taking away my civil rights, my freedom of speech, my freedom of religion and expression."

"Yeah, yeah, yeah... take it off."

"But sir, this is an Iranian airline with a direct flight to Tehran and all I have under this burka is my one-way ticket out of America. I never want to come back to this land of American imperialists. I want to go back to my country where we chop off the hands of thieves."

"Did you say "one-way" ticket out? Direct to Tehran? Oh, so sorry to bother you madam. Have a nice trip." They chop off the hands of thieves? Actually, that's not a bad idea.

That leads me to fashion... wear what you want... you are free to look like an idiot. Why do gangsters wear their pants down to their knees? Is their brain so poisoned by crack that they don't realize how stupid they look? Through my eyes, a burka is totally creepy. However, if there were only two forms of attire on this planet, pants down to my knees or the burka... I'd choose the burka. I guess a burka could have its advantages – I could give my boss the middle finger without getting fired. Or I could become a professional bandit. Recently in South Australia, a man was held up at gunpoint and robbed. The thief was wearing a burka. I hear that the police line-up of five "burka" robbery suspects didn't go too well. And here is another clever idea; a university dean banned the wearing of burkas on campus, stating that males could wear them as disguises to sneak into female dormitories. I like that... great idea. Love the burka!

Why does a pretty girl wear jeans that look as if a pitbull had mauled her? Why do fashion designers make pretty models wear what can only be described as "Halloween costumes" when strutting down the runway? Why do people attending the fashion shows applaud at models in outfits so bizarre no one in their right mind would wear that garb in public? Maybe that's why models don't smile – they feel like fools. Why does someone wear a baseball cap sideways with the price tag still attached to it? Mmmmm... have I filed this complaint before? Oh my... I am on the wrong planet.

"Never argue with a fool -- people might not be able to tell the difference."

FREE RANGE CHICKENS?

Free range chickens – what is that supposed to mean? The first time I saw that label stuck on a pack of drumsticks and wings I figured that was a great deal, so I purchased the chicken and then asked the grumpy cashier for my free stove. This particular cashier had a reputation of being rude and bad-mannered to customers so I intentionally singled her out for my little caper. When she told me that no free range came with the purchase of the chicken, I demanded to know why the store endorsed false advertising. She shot back and suggested that I leave the chicken.

"No," I told her. "I want my free range, and make it a "Magic Chef". She rolled her eyes and got on her microphone. "Manager... manager needed at register No. 4." Up to this point I was just pulling her leg, hoping to make her smile. But her surly attitude pissed me off so I decided to stretch out my little hoax. A skinny little fellow wearing a bow-tie and a tag identifying him as the manager asked if he could help.

"Yeah, this lady won't give me my free stove with the purchase of this chicken."

The manager looked perplexed as he studied the label. In the meantime, a line of unhappy shoppers started forming behind me. All I wanted the manager to do was laugh at my little prank; instead he took the "customer-is-always-right" approach.

"You know sir, this label could be a little deceiving and I'd like to apologize for that. Could I offer you this chicken free as a settlement of our oversight?"

I pretended to be thinking about it as the line of shoppers following me became more restless. The bad-mannered cashier seemed rather disturbed that the manger offered me free chicken. She huffed, she puffed and looked totally fed up.

"OK, I'll take that deal," I said, "but only if you instruct this cashier to smile and be courteous to that long line of customers behind me."

For this I was absolved by the waiting shoppers who awarded me with a round of applause. I waited just long enough to witness the manager scold the grumpy employee about her impolite conduct towards customers. I passed on a sneer and grinned with revenge and left with my chicken. But why free range chicken? I asked my animal-loving wife about this. Teary-eyed, she went on to explain how the average poor chicken is fattened up for the butcher in an enormous chicken coup with thousands of other chickens squawking, pooping and scratching. They can barely move or find nap time due to constant clucking of their fellow foul inmates. Now a free range chicken can run around outside in a fenced area, bask in the sun, be chased by the rooster and peck for bugs in the sand. Ah, what a life... that is until the organic butcher shows up and its judgment day. Whack! There goes the head of the free range chicken. Then the free range feathers are plucked, and the free range guts ripped out. Then it's seasoned, dipped in hot oil and stuffed in a box with coleslaw and French fries. Such is the chronicle of a free range chicken. Does Colonel Sanders use free range chickens? Well, it seems he kills about 40 million birds each year. I teasingly ask my wife what she thinks about Colonel Sanders.

How can I be so cold and unsympathetic? Colonel Sanders is cruel to chickens. Chickens believe he's the devil. What? How do we know what chickens think? Chickens are creatures that function totally on reaction and instinct. In other words, they don't believe anything. The stupid argument continues with my wife supporting the chickens. She hands me a scenario: "Would you rather live cooped up with a thousand other humans or be set free to roam wherever you choose to go?"

"If I were a chicken, either way I end up in the slaughter house. At least in the confinement of the chicken coop I won't be screwed by the rooster before they chop off my head." She huffs in disgust: "You're from another planet so I don't expect any more from you."

The waiter said, "All of our chicken is free range." And I said, "He doesn't look very free there on that plate."
– Joe Bob Briggs

YOU CAN'T FIX STUPID

The Darwin's are out! (Compliments of the Internet). Yes, it's that magical time of year again when the Darwin Awards are bestowed, honoring the least-evolved among the human species.

Here is the glorious winner:

1. When his 38-caliber revolver failed to fire at his intended victim during a hold-up in Provo, Utah would-be robber Jason Ellison did something that can only inspire wonder. He peered down the barrel and tried the trigger again. This time it worked.

And now, the Honorable Mentions:

2. The chef at a hotel in Switzerland lost a finger in a meat-cutting machine. He submitted a claim to his insurance company. The company, expecting negligence, sent out one of its men to have a look for himself. He tried the machine and he also lost a finger. The chef's claim was approved.

3. A man who shoveled snow for an hour to clear a space for his car during a blizzard in Chicago returned with his vehicle to find a woman had taken the space. Understandably, he shot her.

4. After stopping for drinks at an illegal bar, a Zimbabwean bus driver found that the 20 mental patients he was supposed to be transporting from

Harare to Bulawayo had escaped. Not wanting to admit his incompetence, the driver went to a nearby bus stop and offered everyone waiting there a free ride. He then delivered the passengers to the mental hospital, telling the staff that the patients were very excitable and prone to bizarre fantasies. The deception wasn't discovered for three days.

5. A teenager was in the hospital recovering from serious head wounds received from an oncoming train. When asked how he received the injuries, the lad told police that he was simply trying to see how close he could get his head to a moving train before he was hit.

6. A man walked into a Louisiana Circle-K, put a $20 bill on the counter, and asked for change. When the clerk opened the cash drawer, the man pulled a gun and asked for all the cash in the register, which the clerk promptly provided. The man took the cash from the clerk and fled, leaving the $20 bill on the counter. The total amount of cash he got from the drawer... $15. If someone points a gun at you and gives you money, is a crime committed?

7. Seems an Arkansas guy wanted some beer pretty badly. He decided that he'd just throw a cinder block through a liquor store window, grab some booze, and run. So he lifted the cinder block and heaved it over his head at the window. The cinder block bounced back and hit the would-be thief on the head, knocking him unconscious. The liquor store window was made of Plexiglas. The whole event was caught on videotape.

8. As a female shopper exited a South Carolina convenience store, a man grabbed her purse and

ran. The clerk called 9-1-1 immediately, and the woman was able to give them a detailed description of the snatcher. Within minutes, the police apprehended the snatcher. They put him in the car and drove back to the store. The thief was then taken out of the car and told to stand there for a positive ID. To which he replied, "Yes, officer, that's her. That's the lady I stole the purse from."

9. The Ann Arbor News crime column reported that a man walked into a Burger King in Ypsilanti, Michigan at 5 a.m., flashed a gun, and demanded cash. The clerk turned him down because he said he couldn't open the cash register without a food order. When the man ordered onion rings, the clerk said they weren't available for breakfast. The man, frustrated, walked away. *A 5-STAR STUPIDITY AWARD WINNER.

10. When a man attempted to siphon gasoline from a motor home parked on an Atlanta street, he got much more than he bargained for. Police arrived at the scene to find a very sick man curled up next to the motor home near spilled sewage. A police spokesman said that the man admitted to trying to steal gasoline, but he plugged his siphon hose into the motor home's sewage tank by mistake. The owner of the vehicle declined to press charges saying that it was the best laugh he'd ever had.

Remember... They walk among us, they vote and they breed! The people mentioned above are on the right planet.

THE PERFECT JOB

Very few of us on this planet or Coherent are lucky enough to make a career out of a dream. What I mean by this is that most humans go to work because they have to. There are bills to pay and brats to feed. But to actually be working at a job you like, a job you've always dreamed of – those lucky enough are few and far between.

I've always been told that I have the ideal job. I live on a tropical island along the beach and work an average of four hours per day strumming tropical tunes to inebriated tourists who could care less if I'm out of tune and forget my lyrics – oh, what a life! Apart from being on the wrong planet, the Tiki gods have been good to me. My dreams have come true – I've always fantasized about living on an island, spending my days fishing and serenading some Polynesian beauty under a coconut tree. As I enter my golden years I can say much of that dream has come true. Not as reverie as I would have liked, but it's been pretty much a flight of fancy.

I've always wondered how some people do it. They get up at 6 a.m. to sit in traffic for two hours. Then at their workplace most usually hate their boss and co-workers. They watch the clock for lunch hour and constantly check their watch. Then it's back into traffic, a fast food dinner and the next day it starts all over again. I read online that less than half of Americans – 47 percent – are satisfied with their jobs, according to a survey of 5,000 households. Just the thought of a "9-to-5" makes me want to put a revolver to my head. I just can't imagine waking up in the morning and viewing an enticing calm sea, dancing palm fronds and the ascent of a blazing sun while I adjust my tie and shine my genuine alligator shoes and off to the office. I just can't envision that. Though I have no complaints about my occupation I have searched far and wide for the perfect job. What could be better than living on a tropical island and working four hours per day? What would I choose if there is such a thing as an afterlife, when I may be reborn into another planet and begin my life cycle over again? There is no question (in my opinion) the most perfect job is that of a labiaplasty surgeon. What is a labiaplasty surgeon? Well, in layman's terms: a "vagina designer."

Some women are ashamed or embarrassed about the way their genitals look and have the desire to change its appearance. Other times, women want to increase sexual function – a reduction of the labia or clitoral hood can provide greater exposure of the clitoris, allowing for increased stimulation. Occasionally, a woman's vagina is damaged during childbirth, and the labiaplasty procedure is restorative. Some women believe their vagina is either too saggy, baggy or just plain old ugly. Well, I can't imagine any such a thing... I've never seen an ugly vagina yet. However today, I'm Doctor Nowak and you are the customer (the patient) – so let's see what ya got...

"Ohhh, wow... What's wrong with that? Looks lovely, in my opinion."

"I don't care doctor, I want you to fix it... make it smaller... a little tighter... not so flabby."

"Mmmmm... OK, let me have a closer look."

And that's it... that's what I would do every day performing my marvelous 9-to-5 job. I look at, examine, caress and reconstruct vaginas. What a job! If no such occupation was available on Planet Coherent I wouldn't complain about living on Earth as a labiaplasty surgeon. I would look forward going to my office every day. I wouldn't complain about the traffic or the overtime hours. I'd make a ton of money for doing a job that I love. I would, of course, have an assistant, a specialist who would handle the more difficult jobs – like the obese, old and super skinny patients. Of course, he would make more money than I and he would deserve it. Can you imagine the conversation when my assistant sits down at his family table for an evening meal?

Wife: "Hello dear... how was your day in the office?"

"Oh, same old, same old. Miss Jones was back today for her after surgery follow-up."

"Oh, that's nice... how's her vagina looking?"

"Oh same old, same old."

Labiaplasty surgeries are skyrocketing. The average cost for reconstructing a vagina can be around $5,000 to $6,000, so if I'm examining and reconstructing two fresh vaginas per day... wow! What compensation for such a rewarding job. Yes, that would be a dream job. Like any occupation, there could be snags – a medical malpractice lawsuit for example. That's when the vagina business could get a bit "hairy" (no pun intended). Just imagine:

Slimy lawyer: "Your Honor, Dr. Nowak, the director of HVRI (Happy Vagina Reconstruction Institute) failed to provide adequate treatment to my client Miss Jones, resulting in substantial loss of income. Just look at these before and after photos of Miss Jones's vagina."

The Judge: "Mmmmm... which is before and which is after?"

"Your Honor, if you take a very close look you will note that... "

"The court will take a 15-minute recess while I study these photos in my chambers."

30 minutes later

The Judge: "Counselor, I have been studying these two photographs in my bathroom... I mean chambers... and I see little difference in the two images. I'm going to need more evidence than this or prepare to have this civil action discharged. And barrister, you're claiming loss of income. Just what is it your client does for a living?"

"Sir, she is horizontally-inclined."

"What's that?"

"Sir, she is a working girl... a hard working girl."

"Barrister stop beating around the bush (no pun intended). Explain to me: what does your client do for a living?"

Dr. Nowak's attorney: "She's a whore!"

"Objection!"

"Overruled!"

Miss Jones raises her hand. "Your Honor, can I speak?"

"Sure Miss Jones, what do you have to say about all of this?"

"I'd like to make a suggestion, sir. What if you personally view the scene of the alleged crime and you personally examine the damage caused by Dr. Nowak's clinic? Then you will understand why I should be awarded compensatory and punitive damages."

Dr. Nowak's Attorney: "Objection!"

Judge: "Overruled!"

Miss Jones winks at the Judge.

Judge: "Court is adjourned for the weekend. We will resume Monday morning at 9 a.m. – and then I will give you my decision. Please follow me, Miss Jones."

Dr. Nowak's attorney: "Weekend... weekend... but sir, today is only Wednesday!"

"Overruled!"

Like any business being a vagina designer has its ups and downs (no pun intended) – but the rewards would be gratifying, to say the least. I've thought about other jobs that I could possibly pull off. A career fisherman maybe – now that's a good choice. I love to fish. I could spend most of my time at sea far away from humans. No pressure: I decide my own latitude, longitude and attitude; lots of free seafood and no stress. And then, here comes a hurricane... which now decides your latitude and longitude. The declining barometric pressure leads to stress, your boat sinks and soon you wash up drenched on some shore occupied by humans. I love my leisurely time spent fishing, but as a career... No! A movie star, maybe? I'm sure I would have never made it; I don't have the celebrity stubbly-chin look. My blue eyes are usually bloodshot and my "six-pack" abs is just that – a consequence of the latest six-pack. I may even be mauled by young hot babes all the time... no peace. One thing is for sure: you don't have to be handsome or sexy to be a movie star – just look at Woody Allen. Maybe I could be a politician, preacher or lawyer? Never. They lie too much. I have no problem lying about the size of the fish I never caught, my age or my alcohol consumption but to make a career out of lying? Not sure... I don't think it would work considering that I'd have to tell a fresh lie to get out of the last lie that I told because I forgot my original lie.

Recently an Australian state launched a global search for candidates for "the best job in the world" – earning a top salary for lazing around a beautiful tropical island. The job pays $150,000 Australian dollars (U.S. $105,000) annually and includes free airfare from the successful applicant's home country to Hamilton Island on the Great Barrier Reef. In return, the "island caretaker" will be expected to stroll the white sands, soak up the sun, snorkel the reef and maybe clean the pool. I thought about applying for that job, then came to the conclusion... "Been there, done that, got the T-shirt."

Then there are the professional coconut watchers on Suwarrow atoll in the Cook Island chain. Now they have a dream job on a dream island. They don't get paid much, however there's not much to do except watch coconuts and fish... Do you want to apply? For more information read my book "Which Way to the Islands" on Amazon Kindle.

"The reason I talk to myself is because I'm the only one whose answers I accept."
– George Carlin

THE GOLDEN YEARS - BULLSHIT

Why do they call it the golden years? When I wrote the first chapter to this book I had just celebrated my 63rd birthday. Celebration is the wrong word – "exasperation" is a better adage.

> *The Golden Years have come at last,*
> *I cannot see, I cannot pee,*
> *I cannot chew, I cannot screw*
> *My memory shrinks, my hearing stinks,*
> *No sense of smell,*
> *I look like hell,*
> *My body's drooping,*
> *Got trouble pooping.*
> *The Golden Years have come at last,*
> *The Golden Years can kiss my ass.*
> - Author unknown

I recall when I could jog five miles a day in the tropical heat, free dive 30 to 40 feet and chase a grouper into a cave and come back to the surface with the fish on the end of my spear. I used to laugh when older folks warned me – "When you reach 50 everything goes downhill." Never in my life, I would say. At the ripe old age of 61 I finally got my head together; however now my body is falling apart. The doctor leaves a message on my email. Time to come in and pee in a cup, drain a sample of blood, scare you to death about your blood pressure and don't forget to bring your insurance card. My day starts with a cup of coffee that I shouldn't be drinking... bacon and eggs I shouldn't be eating... and a collection of multicolored pills. Let's see... one for gout (the king's disease they call it – LOL) one for cholesterol because I'm eating like a king, one to keep the heart from going out of time, one to keep the blood flowing, one for...? I forgot what that one is for. All I know it's a blue color and makes my wife very happy. The Golden Years... big joke. I am not supposed to eat burgers and fries or consume no more than two beers a day. I'm supposed to steam my grouper instead of frying it, eat lots of green stuff (barf), not smoke that fine $30 Cohiba – not even smell it. If you're feeling frisky and your wife is looking inviting, best make sure your heart can take it. Golden Years? Give me the golden bullet right between my cataract eyes... can't take it no more. There's just too much bad information out there. One doctor says, "Easy on the eggs, they clog up the arteries. Just eat the white part." That makes no sense at all. That would be like having a melted Styrofoam cup for breakfast. Another doctor, Dr. Mehmet Oz to be exact, says make sure you eat one egg a day. He claims this nutritional powerhouse (the egg) does a body good. One egg provides 13 percent of your daily protein requirement and only four percent of the average recommended daily calorie count. Plus, it contains a hefty dose of lutein, an antioxidant that protects your eyes from macular degeneration and UV damage. An egg a day may even help keep Alzheimer's away: the yolk is a significant source of choline, a nutrient that reduces inflammation in the brain. I love eggs, so if it helps prevent Alzheimer's then why not eat four eggs a day? Now the same Dr. Oz that claims eggs are good for you also says that there is arsenic in some apple juice fed to babies! You can't win.

So who do you believe when they say: don't drink alcohol. A New England Journal of Medicine study examining the roles of drinking patterns and heart disease found that after 12 years of follow- up, men who consumed alcohol between three and seven days a week had fewer heart attacks than men who drank once a week. Makes sense to me. Why doesn't the heart disease risk factors affect those Gauloises-smoking, double-cream brie and baguette-eating French? It's gotta be the wine. Then there's vitamin C... all my life I have heard how good vitamin C is for you. I'd drink my orange juice, eat strawberries and pop a huge vitamin C pill every day. After all, your body does not make or retain vitamin C so any extra will simply be flushed out of your body in your urine. Then, just when I'm feeling healthy, a new study in some medical journal makes an announcement that too much vitamin C can cause diarrhea, nausea, vomiting, heartburn, abdominal cramps, headache, insomnia, kidney stones. Damn. Can you believe it? Doctors, please make up your minds. Then there's a new medication for blood pressure – however this new amazing pill could cause diarrhea, nausea, vomiting, heartburn, abdominal cramps, headache, insomnia and kidney stones. Damn. Can you believe it? That pisses me off.

And how about this one? Don't eat white rice or white bread, it's really bad for you. No rice and bread? That's so dumb. You need carbs to survive and function. As long as you exercise regularly, you can eat them and not give a second thought to it. Ask most any healthy, elderly Asian and they will say white rice is a staple in their diet. White rice turns to glucose after ingestion and quickly used for energy (excess will be stored as fat!). One younger Asian says, "I consume white rice only 30 minutes prior to my workout and maybe with 15 to 20 minutes after an intense workout. This allows my body to replenish glycogen cells and ensures minimal fat conversion. Seen a fat Japanese person lately? (Sumo wrestlers don't count). Japan has the oldest life expectancy in the world. That means people in Japan live a really, really long time. Men live to 79 years old. Women live a little over 86 years old. What in the world causes Japanese people to live so long? Many things including rice; rice is eaten with almost everything and is high in nutrients. At the time of this writing the "World's Oldest Person" according to Guinness World Records and the Gerontology Research Group is Misao Okawa,115, of Osaka, Japan, born March 5, 1898. She became the world's oldest person on June 12, 2013 with the passing of Jiroemon Kimura, 116, of Kyotango, Japan.

Just when I'm getting depressed with all the medication perplexity, there is finally some good, reliable news. New research shows that men who make love regularly are up to 45 percent less likely to develop fatal heart conditions than those who only have sex once a month or less. Now we're talking! Since 1987, scientists at the New England Research Institute in Massachusetts have studied the sexual activity of over 1,000 men between the ages of 40 and 70. The results of the study, which were recently published in the American Journal of Cardiology, show that men who did the deed at least twice a week were significantly less likely to suffer from heart disease. Glory Hallelujah! What wonderful news! And there's more. The National Cancer Institute showed that men who ejaculated at least five times a week were less likely to get prostate cancer. And, if that's not enough, researchers at Wilkes University in Pennsylvania even proved that having sex just once or twice a week in the winter can reduce the risk of catching a cold or flu.

"C'mon honey... slip out of that skirt, turn down the lights and keep me healthy."

"No, I got a headache."

"But what about my heart, my prostate? Do you want me to catch the flu?"

"But it's that time of the month."

"Well, then how about frying me some eggs?"

Then I could choose to be a vegan like my daughter. No butter, no fries, no steak, no cheese, no ribs, no bacon. She will, however, share a bottle of tequila with me – top-shelf only. Doesn't the body need protein? I hear so much about tofu, a preference of vegetarians, that it's a good source of protein like bacon, beef, chicken and hot dogs. So I did a blind taste test. Tofu in one bowl and nothing in another bowl – I couldn't tell the difference. OK, I didn't want to be to judgmental too hastily, so I tried again. Tofu in one bowl and Gummy Bears in the other... we have a winner – Gummy Bears.

If everyone in the U.S. and Canada became a vegetarian, millions of people who work at Burger King, McDonald's, Wendy's, KFC and Pizza Hut would be out of a job. The government would have to hand out food stamps to the unemployed. Welfare lines would be a mile long and what could they get with their food stamps? Cauliflower and tofu? Farmers wouldn't have enough land to grow all the veggies and fast-food executives would have to find new jobs like picking apples, and then all the illegal Mexicans would be out of work, and then they would go back to Mexico and get a job at Taco Bell and then... just what is my point? I don't know. I'm not from this planet.

"The West wasn't won on salad."

PETA

I love animals, actually. I have no choice. My wife has four dogs, two horses and two cats. No question: a dog is man's (or girl's) best friend. If you can say honestly that deep down in your heart you have no prejudice against creed, color, religion or politics... you are almost as good as a dog! If I had to choose between living in an apartment complex which housed a bunch of humans or living at a dog pound... I'd choose the latter. And then there's PETA (People for the Ethical Treatment of Animals), the largest animal rights organization in the world with more than two million members and supporters. PETA focuses its attention on the four areas in which the largest numbers of animals suffer the most intensely for the longest periods of time: on factory farms, in the clothing trade, in laboratories and in the entertainment industry. They also work on a variety of other issues, including the cruel killing of beavers, birds and other "pests" as well as cruelty to domesticated animals. Why would someone kill a beaver? A beaver is not a pest - I love beavers.

PETA works through public education, cruelty investigations, research, animal rescue, legislation, special events, celebrity involvement and protest campaigns. They are also well-known for their shocking adverts with some of the world's most famous people posing naked to help boost their animal rights message. Hey, I see no problem with *Playboy* model Joanna Krupathis standing nude and furless in the middle of a busy downtown street with the message: "I'd rather go naked than wear fur." Love it... great marketing. However, PETA may have gone too far with a campaign that suggests those who fish or spearfish may be attacked or killed by a great white as "payback" for sport fishing. Their poster shows a shark eating a severed human leg with a blood-stained slogan: "Payback is Hell", which aims to shock people into turning vegan. I think about that "payback" poster every time I descend on a coral reef to shoot a grouper or snapper for my dinner, the poster haunts me. I always wonder if the groupers, snappers and lobsters have gotten together and finally put out a contract on me... if they would hire that great white to do me in. I guess they are justified to do so, considering all the fresh seafood I've consumed in my lifetime. When I ascend with or without a fish on my spear I do so in a spin: always looking around just in case the finned assassin has found me in this massive ocean.

Animal rights are a good thing, I support it, but PETA (in my opinion) simply goes too far sometimes – they can piss me off. Most of us want meat. If we're not supposed to eat animals, how come they're made out of meat? Why doesn't PETA protest Mother Nature when she lets a lion runs down some innocent zebra, or when a hawk plummets on a cute little field mouse or an orca swallows a seal? It's simply Mother Nature at work. It's my nature to fish – even if I die doing it. A bad day of fishing is better than a good day of anything else.

Dear PETA:

I love dogs, birds and pussycats so don't tell me what I can and can't eat and don't have me terrified every time I partake in my favorite sport – spearfishing. Spear the fish or hook the fish: a dead fish is a dead fish.

PETA is especially hard on Colonel Sanders who slaughters millions of fouls annually. Now, get real, PETA. We've discussed this before. Do chickens really know that their sole purpose on Earth is to end up in a deep fryer? It remains unclear what exactly goes on in the minds of chickens, which are raised at a rate of a billion birds per year to satisfy human consumption demands. Dr. Christine Nicol, who studies chicken intelligence, reflected, "They may be 'bird brains,' but we need to redefine what we mean by 'bird brains'. Chickens have shown us they can do things people didn't think they could do." There are definitely hidden depths to chickens, or so she says.

I find it totally bizarre that someone would want to make a career out of studying chicken intelligence. There are plenty of pedophiles and serial killers that these same doctors could be experimenting with. Brainy or stupid chickens, I don't care ... I want my spicy Hooters.

Chickens are always causing trouble. One sultry foul posed for Wendy's in a pin-up-style photo, lounging seductively in the food section of the *New York Times* along with a story on the appeal of crispy, savory chicken skin. "When I saw it I just couldn't believe that an editor of *The New York Times* would find it acceptable," moaned PETA's founder and President Ingrid Newkirk. "It's right offensive, not just to people who care about animals but to almost everyone. It's a plucked, beheaded young chicken in a sexy pose," she said. Oh for goodness sake, get a life Ingrid. Get your butt out of the office and do some real animal rights work. Go pick on gangsters and rappers who train pit bulls to rip each other apart. Go to the Orient where they deep-fry dogs, cats and exotic birds.

I saw the sultry chicken ad, loved it. It turned me on, so I went to Wendy's and purchased a few bags of sexy chicken just to piss PETA off. I sure hope Wendy's didn't apologize to PETA. I hate it when people do that. Why apologize for doing no wrong? I recall reporter Nina Totenberg openly apologized for using the phrase, "Christmas party" while speaking on the program "Inside Washington". Discussing the omnibus spending bill that was rejected, she recalled a conversation with government defense officials regarding their budgets, a conversation that took place at a Christmas party. However, before she used the party's adjective, she asked for forgiveness for invoking the "holiday" term. She said – *"Well, these agencies, including the Defense Department, don't know how much money they've got and for what.*

And I was at – forgive the expression – a Christmas party at the Department of Justice and people actually were really worried about this." Why did she apologize for using the words "Christmas party"? Why ? I don't mean to be petty, but F#@K them if they don't like the words "Christmas Party". Then there's Robin Robinson, an anchor at Fox Chicago. She made a comment, "There is no Santa" on a segment about managing gift expectations of children. She caught total crap from a bunch of angry soccer moms and the next day she apologized – why? She was being truthful. There is no F#@&KING Santa. And what kid still young enough to believe in Santa, sits around in the evening and watches Fox News? Wake up, soccer moms, your kids could care less about what a Fox News anchor has to say. Right now your kids are in their room playing Grand Theft Auto or shooting Father Christmas on a video game. Planet Coherent please beam me up... I'm on the wrong planet!

ARE ANIMALS SMARTER THAN PEOPLE?

Of course they are. Humans question this theory, Coherents acknowledge it. Just take a dog for example. Love him and feed him he'll stick by your side always. Love and feed your wife, she'll run off with a richer guy or some young stud. Love and feed your kids, they become adults and want to borrow money. A dog has no color prejudice, be you black, white, green or yellow; treat him good and a dog will love you back. He doesn't want your money, just feed him and pet him that's all that is required for his loyalty. If it's 90 degrees outside he's smart enough to sleep in the shade, where some humans walk around wearing a hoody. He can look up a girl's dress and not be charged with sexual harassment; instead the girl will pet him and give him a bone (no pun intended).

The Jordan family had just moved to Charleston, S.C., with their seven-month-old son, Finn. They were a working mom and dad so they hired baby sitter Alexis Khan. Being the good parents they are, they did a background check on Alexis and she came up clean. Initially they trusted Alexis but as time moved along the Jordan's started getting bad vibes, not from the sitter but from their family pooch 'Killian'.

"We started to notice that our dog was very defensive of our son when Alexis would come in the door," said Benjamin Jordan.

"He was very aggressive towards her and a few times we actually had to physically restrain our dog from going after her."

Naturally this made the parents suspicious, so they decided to put an iPhone under the couch to record what was happening in the house. And then came the shocker, the audio recording captured the sounds of the sitter cussing at and slapping the baby when he cried. Khan was taken into police custody and pleaded guilty to assault and battery. She'll be placed on a child abuse registry so she won't be allowed to work with kids again. What a light sentence for such a sickening, slob child abuser. If it wasn't for Killian, who is obviously much smarter that Alexis, she may have never been caught.

Then there's the homing pigeon, set him free and he can find his home some 1,000 miles away without the use of a GPS, maps, radar or road sign. Now that's smart for a bird brain.

Ants can reproduce by cloning. Humans are still working on it.

Elephants are huge and often sluggish. However an elephant can track up to 30 members of their family with its long, unusual looking nose by sniffing out their scent and building a mental map of where they are. Humanoid parents can't keep track of their teenagers on a Saturday night.

Much has been said about the intelligence of chimps, with some people even claiming they're geniuses. Chimps have an amazing photographic memory capable for numerical recollection. Presented with the same sequence of numbers, small chimps could recall them, outperforming humans. Chimps don't have to depend on calculators or smart phones to recollect numbers. So next time someone calls you a "chimp", take it as a compliment.

Though not officially smarter than humans "yet", dolphins have recently been declared the world's second most intelligent creatures (after Coherents). A zoologist from Emory University in Atlanta, Georgia, has even gone as far to say that their "neuroanatomy suggests psychological continuity between humans and dolphins." Their brains are only second in size to a Coherent. Unfortunately their intellect can cost them their freedom when they end up in some marine park entertaining humans with small brains. How long will these clever animals put up with human abuse?

On my planet zoos and marine mammal parks are outlawed. On my planet animal cruelty is as serious a crime as the murder of a human, except we don't send you to prison; you are locked away at the Predatory Correctional Facility. Here humans in violation of animal cruelty laws are locked up and guarded by chimps. They are fed by gorillas and showered by a snot-filled elephant's nose. There's not a human in sight except for the delivery of food – food to feed the animals. Anything left over is for the prisoners, the humans. Try not to escape; the facility is encircled with three razor wire fences. Residing within these layer of fences are dogs that have been abused, dogs looking for revenge. There is some form of entertainment at the feeding hall. Convicts are required to jump through hoops before being fed. It's real cheerful place – but unfortunately only found on my planet.

What are you thinking right now? That I'm totally insane with my suggestion of a Predatory Correction Facility? Well consider this, for a second. In the state of Illinois the torturing or killing of an animal vertebrate (animal with a backbone) can bring a fine of $5,000 or one year in prison. Now that's the maximum sentence which is rarely carried out. So if you are sent to prison (which is rare) for one year, for intentionally killing or torturing a dog, cat, horse or parrot you will be out in six months for good behavior. Of course you'll behave in prison because you are a coward and there are no animals to kill. Planet Earth has its share of animal abusing cowards.

In Stanfordville, New York, Stanley Jablonka decided a deaf and blind Great Dane was aggressive and rabid when the dog barked at his brother. So pretending to be an animal expert he shoots the Dane and decapitates him with an axe. He was not found guilty of animal cruelty; rather he was convicted for the inhumane destruction of a dog and was sentenced to six months in jail. Animal cruelty or inhumane destruction of a dog, what's the f***ing difference? He was also found guilty of criminal possession of a firearm and criminal mischief. As a convicted felon, Jablonka wasn't allowed to own weapons. In addition to the six-month jail sentence, Jablonka has to pay a $1,000 fine, plus a $205 court surcharge. That's not the end of the story. Jablonka's lawyer intends to appeal the verdict. OMG what a f***ed up planet. Shoot the lawyer and send Jablonka to my planet. The guards at the Predatory Correction Facility are waiting for him.

Now what about fish? I heard an old fisherman in the Exumas once say: "Fish no fool." I'll parrot those words "Fish no fool" – some can be amazingly smart. Before I tell you about my fish experience I need to mention again that PETA (in my opinion) has crossed the line with their 'No hunting, No fishing stance'. PETA talks out of both sides of its mouth. Besides the good work they do, they are also a hypocritical animal rights group that has killed 29,398 domestic animals. What, you say? Check it out yourself at www.petakillsanimals.com. No hunting or fishing? That is totally ridiculous; man cannot live on bread and rum alone.

Now back to fishing. In my much younger days living in the Bahamas, I used to earn extra money by scrubbing the bottom of yachts to free them of algae and barnacles. Once the worm-filled barnacles floated to the bottom the action would begin. Small tropical fish would come out of nowhere and pick for the worms. The feeding frenzy of the smaller fish would attract larger fish and soon the delicious, flavorsome Mutton Snapper would make the scene. The Mutton Snapper is a shy, skittish fish and not that easy to spear or hook. During my cleaning duties I would notice several huge snappers swimming around me, some so close I could almost touch them. They were there to ingest the smaller fish eating on the worms.

Ahh, I thought to myself , Mutton fish for dinner, this is going to be a turkey shoot. I dashed back to my cottage and grabbed my Hawaiian sling. The Hawaiian sling is a device used in spearfishing. The sling operates much like a bow and arrow on land: energy is stored in rubber tubing rather than a wooden or fiberglass shaft. I made my way back into the water and settled the sling and spear in the sand under the yacht. I carried on with my work of cleaning the boat's bottom and within no time the smaller fish were back, soon followed by the snappers. This time, however, the snapper stayed some good length away from me. Strange, I thought, earlier I could almost kiss them. I continued my work but the snapper never moved in close enough for me to take a shot. Later that day I told this story to one of the old fishermen cleaning his catch by the village dock.

"They saw your spear, that's why they stayed away," he said.

"Absurd," I responded. "It's nothing but a fish, with a small brain."

He invited me on his small wooden ship. "Come aboard. Let me show you something."

He diced some bait and tossed it under the dock. The water started to boil with small fish going into turmoil to get their share of the scraps. He passed me a line with a baited hook and instructed me to catch one of the fish. He proceeded in tossing more bait. I dropped my hook and before it hit bottom I had caught a nice size grunt, big enough to fry.

The demonstration confused me.

"And what is the point you are trying to make?" I queried.

Without saying another word he tossed more scraps in the water and all the fish were gone. Nothing – not even a crab.

"You see young man, out of the hundreds of feeding fish, you pulled one out of the water. Now you'll not get another one at this spot for the rest of the day. Fish no fool."

It was an interesting lesson but I was still skeptical. "It's a fish. They can't be that smart." So, before dark I dove back into the sea and in the sand beneath the yacht I buried my spear. I covered it well to make sure nothing of the spear was exposed. The following morning after breakfast I went to finish my job. Garbed in my dive gear and I went back to work scrapping barnacles. Within minutes the small fish moved in for their breakfast. They were soon followed by several huge snapper which I observed coming from the distance. And in the distance they stayed, gracefully circling some 20 feet away.

"Impossible," I thought. "It's a fish. They can't possibly know that my Hawaiian sling was buried beneath me in the sand."

I was slipping on my job and not getting my work done. Mother Nature was starting to piss me off. This experiment must end once and for all. I removed my weighty dive gear and retrieved my spear from the sand. I climbed up the dock ladder and placed my spear on the bow of the yacht. I dove back into the sea and by the time the bubbles had cleared my face mask there he was – a huge, shiny red Mutton fish within two feet of my mask. I could see the yellow of his iris and he could see my amazement through my goggles.

As if to say, "Thank you, now it's time for you to go back to work", he swam back to the exact spot where I had buried my spear and patiently waited for his breakfast. Yes..."fish no fool". Imagine a planet with just people , how nice is that?

"Horse sense is the thing a horse has which keeps it from betting on people."
– W. C. Fields

SCIENTIST INSULT ANIMALS

Why do brainy people use silly words to describe something simple? That pisses me off. Take the Christmas Island red crab. Scientists call it a Gecarcoidea natalis. What's with that? A crab is a crab. Take the monkey. In scientific words it can be described as a primate of the Haplorrhini suborder and simian infraorder. Why turn four letters into 34? To a simple Coherent, a monkey is a monkey and a crab is a crab. To an intellectual scientist, a monkey should be a monkey and a crab should be a crap, so why not keep it that way and save some memory in your computer? A Geococcyx californianus is a road runner and a Coleonyx variegatus is a gecko. Just imagine reading to your children:

"And the Geococcyx californianus ate the Coleonyx variegatus."

Talk about turning your kids into a case of Attention Deficit Disorder. Imagine watching your favorite Warner Brothers cartoon – its not the Wile Coyote show, it's the Wile Canis latrans Geococcy californianus show. Reading up on the subject it seems that the reason for the perplexing names is because a monkey in India is a different monkey as found in Africa. A lousy excuse in my opinion, a monkey is still a monkey. Just call it an African monkey or an Indian monkey. Don't call it a "predominantly herbivorous eponymous genus" – a gorilla.

I wonder when out in the field do scientist use these pointless words?

"Hey, Doctor Albert, look up! In that Fraxinus excelsior there's an Ichthyophaga eating an Ichthyophaga paraphyletic."

Why not just say, "Look up in the tree, there's an eagle eating a fish."

"There are plenty of smart people who get nowhere."
– Paul Graham

WHY DO THEY DO THAT?
THE FLAIRING BARTENDERS

My wife and I are on a weekend getaway on the island of Little Cayman. The temp is in the mid-80s, a few puffs of clouds and the lagoon looks so clear and enticing I want to drink it. Bottom line: I need a drink. We stroll up to the Tiki bar to order a few cool concoctions. The place was a hectic mix of fake boobs, shiny SPF-coated bodies and inebriated ex-patriots watching the football game on the big screen. That pisses me off – why would anyone put a TV in their beach bar?

"Good-day, Mr. Bartender, can you please fix me a gin and tonic with lots of lime and my wife will go touristy with a rum punch."

This simple request led to flying bottles, a juggling act, sliding a glass down his back and a Michael Jackson moonwalk. The bar patrons applaud. I roll my eyes – **I was not impressed.**

"You want the top-shelf sir or our house?" asked the juggling bartender.

"Top-shelf? What the hell is that? I want gin, she wants rum."

"On the rocks – or straight up?"

"It's near 90 degrees – why would I want it straight up? On ice please, lots of ice!"

The bottle-slinging continues and everyone claps with approval. That pisses me off.

"Excuse me, if my wife and I wanted a circus act we would have vacationed in Las Vegas, just a drink, please." My sarcasm didn't faze him.

"Well sir," he said. "When you go to Vegas make sure you come see me at the International Flairing Contest."

'Flair' is the art of juggling bottles and flipping glasses in the air and pouring drinks in athletic poses. It's Tom Cruise in "Cocktail". These bartenders are jugglers and part magicians, making a performance art out of one of the oldest professions in the world: bartending. They're much like a chef in a Japanese steakhouse who juggles knives, eggs and shrimp.

"You're going to Vegas to flip bottles? Well, get ready for some major competition. They have Siegfried & Roy and Wayne Newton."

Still not intimidated, he let fly three bottles into the air and shoots back:

"Well, I think Roy was eaten by a tiger and Wayne is more than likely in an old folk's home."

Ouch... for this old man, that was below the belt. Is this guy forgetting I'm the customer? Before I had a chance to snap back, there was my drink: tall, cold – and adorned with a flower and umbrella.

"Excuse me, Mr. Bartender. I have no need for the flower and umbrella. Could I trade that for an extra shot of gin?"

"Sir, I'm not a bartender. I am a mixologist." he says.

I was about to say, "You're a show- off", when he topped my glass with a double shot of Beefeater.

"Mr. Mixologist, could I have some extra lime please?"

That was a mistake – limes were flying through the air and before one reached my glass it was cut Samurai-style into four sections. I could not take anymore, so I asked for my check. "It's complimentary sir, since you didn't enjoy the show – no charge."

No charge, I don't pay.... NICE. I felt victorious. I had outsmarted the young man with spiky hair. My lovely wife said nothing, but I know her; we're like two peas in a pod – I know what's on her mind:

"Just give me a damn drink."

Yeah, that's my girl!

We strolled back down to the shoreline, and before we had settled in our lounge chairs my wife trekked back to the beach bar.

When she returned I asked: "What happened? Did you leave something?"

"No, I gave him a $30 tip – he was HOT."

Damn, that pisses me off.

LEAF BLOWERS

If I ever forget that I'm on the wrong planet (which is rare) the leaf blower is one of the things that will bring me back to reality. They are so horribly annoying – blowing leaves from one side of the garden to another so that Mother Nature can blow them back! Whoever invented this irritating piece of machinery should be blown away. Whoever sells it should be robbed (daily) and whoever uses it should be whacked across the head.

The leaf blower pollutes the air with noise and fumes. A gasoline-powered leaf blower generates as much tailpipe emissions in one hour as an automobile does over 350 miles. We need raw materials to make it, crude oil to run it and idiots to use it. Yes, idiots – and that we have plenty of on this Planet Earth. In fact, the leaf blower is the perfect idiot apparatus.

Sacramento's city code states: "Every person in the city is entitled to live in an environment free from excessive, unnecessary or offensive noise levels." It is so printed that the normally acceptable ambient noise level in residential areas is no more than 60 dB; 60-70 is conditionally acceptable; and higher levels are normally unacceptable. The decibel scale is logarithmic – each increase of 10, say 60 to 70, represents a noise 10 times louder. The average blower measures 70-75 dB at a distance of 50 feet, according to a manufacturer's lobbyist.

blowers are routinely used less than 50 feet from pedestrians and neighboring homes that may be occupied by home workers, retirees, day sleepers, children, the ill or disabled, and pets. (There's something to complain about PETA). Is it really worth manufacturing such an irritating, noise-making and pollution-causing gadget – just to blow leaves back and forth? There's even an "I hate Leaf Blowers" Facebook page. I knew eventually I'd find an excuse to become part of the social network.

What's wrong with a rake and broom? "Nothing," says grandmother Diane Wolfberg of Los Angeles. In three tests involving gas-powered leaf blowers and battery-powered leaf blowers, Diane cleaned several areas using rakes or brooms faster than any of the battery-powered blowers and almost as fast as the gas-powered leaf blowers and she did a better job in cleaning them. And let's consider the dangerous chemicals. Leaf blowers spread dust, dirt, animal droppings, herbicides and pesticides into your air, over your cars and into the windows of your home. Because of leaf blowers, we use more valuable water because everyone in the neighborhood has to wash their car after the leaves have zigzagged pollution across the yards. Another reason why leaf blowers are bad for your health is because you only burn about 10 percent of the calories using a leaf blower as compared to when you use a rake and broom. In the tropics leaf blowers are an extra annoyance. Money-spending tourists sit on the beach listening to seabirds and waves lapping on the shore when here comes some lazy slob blowing coconut fronds that won't move. Airborne sand sticks to sun screened bodies and clouds up the clear water. By the time you complain to management your beach bag, iPod and cell phone is full of sand and seaweed. You demand a discount on your room and early the next morning the gardener is back blowing plastic solo cups off your cabana porch while you attempt to heal a rum-drenched hangover in a nearby hammock. I've been there, done that – and it pisses me off.

I believe people who enjoy working with leaf blowers think they're some sort of Rambo. Why use a sissy rake when you can strap some contraption on your back, wear goggles and blow the crap out of ants and butterflies? Just like Rambo with his bazooka blowing up the Vietcong, having their body parts fly about the jungle. I hate leaf blowers. They should be outlawed. They are outlawed on Planet Coherent.

TIPPING

There's perhaps no aspect of good manners more perplexing than tipping. The idea behind tipping is simple; it's to show appreciation for good service. Having worked in hotels most of my career I know many bar and restaurant employees who depend on tips. I have no problem leaving a tip, even a fat one now and then. However, in some instances, tipping is completely unnecessary and too complicated. I go to one particular restaurant on a regular basis. I like everything about it: the staff is great, the food is excellent and the quiet seashore atmosphere is perfect for this recluse. I do have one regular grievance... the 15 percent gratuity they automatically add onto my bill before I have a chance to leave the 20 percent tip that I was going to leave for the nice experience. Then, on top of that, they always leave an extra line under the total for an additional tip that I may want to leave over the 15 percent involuntary tip. If I don't leave the extra tip I'm a cheapskate. If I add on another 5 percent that would be the 20 percent I was going to leave anyway. So now they have the 20 percent that I was going to happily put down, but 15 percent of that they added without my approval. Now if I only leave another five percent voluntarily, it makes me seem like a miser because technically five percent is all I gave as a tip – the other 15 percent doesn't count because I didn't give it...they took it. You see my point?

It even gets more confusing if the service was lousy or the waiter was surly – they still take the 15 percent. Now, that pisses me off. If you leave no tip due to an overcooked steak, that should be your right – however an overcooked steak is not the fault of a friendly waiter. If you complain to the manager about an overcooked steak prepared by a lousy chef, yet you leave the friendly waiter a nice tip, you may not never want to come back again as there'd be no telling what the chef may put in your soup. I'd rather the establishment just sell me a steak for 20 percent more and forget the tip all together. Then, instead of a tip line at the end of my bill I'd like to see a subtraction line – leave it up to me, the customer, the consumer of your fare, to judge my experience. In other words, I will deduct from the extra 20 percent should I need to – rather than have you attach 15 percent if you want to.

Traditionally, in French Polynesia, tipping has been contrary to the Tahitian custom of hospitality. It is neither required nor expected. However, if you receive particularly good service from someone the gesture will be appreciated. Mind you, they may not accept it but you will not be insulting them either. Wow, isn't that nice? I've been to Polynesia often so I can confirm that tipping etiquette. In New Zealand, staff is very excited when tipped for excellent service but they're not used to the experience of tipping. In a travel article I read, one server asked his manager what to do with "the extra" added on a good-sized bill. Kind of nice, isn't it? The difference is that New Zealanders are paid closer to a "living wage" than much of the U.S. and Caribbean islands. So, in the Pacific, gratuity is really just that: appreciation for the good service. On Planet Coherent, my planet, the word 'tip' does not exist. We simply get rid of bad chefs and surly servers. No, they don't get fired; they end up in the kitchen washing dishes. As for good chefs and pleasant servers, they have a heftier salary than the rest.

"The British tourist is always happy abroad as long as the natives are waiters."
– Robert Morley

THE PUKE MOVIES

I'm getting sick of it... it makes me wanna barf. It seems that in every film I see these days there is a scene with someone throwing up. Why? OK, I guess now and then a scene calls for it, as in "The Exorcist". Now, that spray of continuous green vomit was classic, only to be outdone by Clint Eastwood's classic non-vomit scene in the movie Dirty Harry. Remember? Harry Callahan goes into a diner for a morning cup of coffee. When he discovers a robbery in the diner, he kills the robbers in a shoot-out. However, a surviving robber grabs the fleeing waitress, holds a gun to her head, and threatens to shoot. Instead of backing off, Harry points his huge .44 Magnum into the man's face at point-blank range and dares him to shoot, saying with clenched teeth, "Go ahead, make my day." I love that scene. As I've said before, Harry Callahan is definitely from my planet. Now, no disrespect intended Mr. Eastwood. On my planet that scene would have been slightly different. You would have blown the guy's head off and then said, "Wow, you just made my day."

It seems every Hollywood director since "The Exorcist" is attempting to outdo that famous horror flick with better, more well-defined regurgitates. Green spew from the mouth has advanced to yellow slime mixed with corn, beans and a fountain of nasal drip. Give it a break already! Now the Jackass movies are another exception. In "Jackass 3" (in 3-D) they throw up in the camera. And if that isn't realistic enough, check out the scene in Jackass 2 where the guy drinks a glass of horse semen – that's even better than the 3-D vomit scene. That made me sick, I had to vomit.

With the exception of "The Exorcist", "Jackass" and a few others, there's just no need for all the puke... the director is only regurgitating what the last movie forgot to throw up. I want to see more naked stuff – not really all nude, just the enticing stuff like Sharon Stone in "Basic Instinct". I've seen the 129-minute film five times and I've watched the famous eight-minute interrogation scene 50 times. On a different subject, what's with the scene-skipping thing in so many movies these days? The average brain can't handle it... one moment the actor is in present time and next he goes back in time and before the movie ends he's in the future. Why do the directors do that? Their job is to entertain me, not confuse me. They may know the sequence of events in their story, which is down on script, but I never get it because often there is no succession to the plot. I am not attempting to be a movie critic – well maybe I am – but I just can't stand it when I'm waiting for something to happen and the film fades to black and the credits start rolling. Damn, that pisses me off. Not on my planet.

I just watched a film titled *"Mulholland Drive"*. The Rotten Tomatoes reviewers gave it an 88 percent rating, so I figured it would be half good – not! Why did the girl have all that money in her purse? Why did the two main characters get up in the middle of the night to hear the club singer? And then the singer passes out on stage, but yet she's still singing? It's a shame that two beautiful actors, Naomi Watts and Laura Harring, are wasted in this waste of time. The lesbian scenes were OK... However, if the director had just inserted more porn with these lovely ladies, I may see the sense in renting this flick again. "Southland Tale" is another waste of film... I left the cinema saying, "Why?" Worst of all (in my opinion) was "Inland Empire". That film, by the way, is by the same director as "Mulholland Drive", David Lynch. I can't believe they pay this guy a huge salary to pick snippets of rejected film off the editing floor and tape them together for a Hollywood production. On my planet we would have thrown the entire production in the nearest dumpster and then hired Linda Blair to vomit green puke all over it. C'mon, David Lynch – what's with the people in the rabbit costumes? What is it you are trying to put across? Then again, who am I to judge art? Art is what some movie buffs call this type of cinematography. Those supporters of bad film are on the right planet and I hope they stay here.

EARTHLINGS SAY TOO MUCH STUPID

Let's start with television reporters. They irritate me with their "lost-for-words" inquiries. They have a mike in their hand, someone douses them with make-up, the spotlights go on and then they ask such stupid questions.

"Aside from the gunshot, did you enjoy the play, Mrs. Lincoln?"

Here's one that's more up to date – a reporter interviewing Tom Chars, a burn victim whose face is completely bandaged with the exception of a small slit in the mouth area.

Reporter: "Tell me sir, for our audience... how did it feel to be running from that burned building with your hair on fire."

Tom: "Ummm... I... umm, ouch..."

Reporter: "So third-degree burns must really hurt?"

Tom: "What?"

Reporter: "Is your family upset over this situation?"

Tom: "F** k you!"

Reporter: "Do you plan on suing the building owners because they had no sprinkler system, fire alarm or extinguishers?"

Though this is a made-up story it is basically a fictional example of the often dense, on-the-spot live coverage just to fill air time. On my planet reporters have the right to be dumb, but they are not allowed to ask dump questions. Tourists however, are allowed to ask dumb questions, we need their money.

"Hey, how far is the water from the beach?"

"How long is Seven Mile Beach?"

"How many times today will they have the sunset party?"

"Where do the homeless people live on this island?"

"Is this island completely surrounded by water?"

"Do I have to get wet to swim with the dolphins?"

Then there's the divorce lawyers:

"So sir, your wife is asking for 50 percent of everything that the two of you own, plus an additional $2,000 per month in alimony and let's not forget child support of $3,000 per month, the four horses... oh, and her legal fees... are you willing to agree to that?"

Client: "Oh sure, I'm jumping for joy. She's been screwing the stable boy for the last six months, I'm sleeping at Motel 6 and now I need to get a third job to pay for it all. Of course, I'm ecstatic. Why not give her my jeep also? I don't mind riding a bicycle."

Lawyer: "Well, if you insist... we can..."

Client: "No, you $500-per-hour moron – that was sarcasm. I want you to sue her, have her electrocuted, hung... whatever it takes. I want revenge... and I don't want that stable boy sleeping in my bed!"

Lawyer, grinning with delight: "Of course, sir. This case is a sure winner (he doesn't say for who). Now I need a $1,000 retainer."

Client: "I just left you a retainer check yesterday!"

Lawyer: "But we have been in this meeting for two hours... that's $1,000."

I wonder what Shakespeare meant when he said, "Let's kill all the lawyers."

Back to the same client and lawyer four months later:

"Your Honor, this is a most unusual situation. My client is asking his ex-wife for $5,000 per month, plus his legal fees."

"Why is that counselor?"

"For pain and suffering, sir, for negligence. He's been hurt as you can see – he needs compensation of $5,000 per month, plus legal fees."

"I see he's in a wheelchair. What happened?"

"Sir, he went to deliver his ex-wife her monthly alimony and child support check of $5,000. In the process, he slipped on horse manure and broke his leg and suffered a concussion. Had the stable boy cleaned up the mess in the barn this would not have happened."

"Counselor, it seems like you should be making the claim against the stable boy."

"We would sir, but immigration has deported him back to Argentina."

"Counselor, do you have any proof of you client's injuries?"

"Sir, just look at him... he has a cast on his leg, a bruise on his arm and a bandage on his head."

"And without a medical report I have no evidence to confirm your client's injuries – this could be a sham."

"A sham... a sham... Sir, if you don't believe me, ask him yourself."

"No counselor, you ask him. He's your client."

"But sir, isn't that a bit out of the ordinary to openly ask my client private, privileged, confidential information in an open court?"

"He can whisper in your ear. Ask him or I'll charge you with contempt of court."

"Me sir? Here in open court?"

"Ask him counselor or I'll have the bailiff take you away. If your client is being truthful about his injuries and you are being truthful about his injuries and you are not attempting to commit perjury in this court and considering that I have no medical record, ask him."

"Your Honor, sir. I'd... I'd... like to strike the next question that I will pose to my client."

YES, PEOPLE SAY THE DUMBEST THINGS.

Then there's CNN's Nancy Grace – she says the dumbest things. I don't know what's dippier, her hair or her opinions. She might know the law, but it is so much better for her show and ratings to act like a know-it-all, better-than-you. She brings on guests, and does not let them get a word in edgewise. She provokes anger and plays judge and jury and she certainly inflames many, including me. I'm all for victim's rights but she has, what some called a "lynch mob attitude". Why do I watch her? I don't anymore, especially since she started talking about her twins, Lucy and John – that pisses me off. Then she gets these fake tears in her eyes and starts whining. This is followed by photographs of them eating their cereal or opening Christmas gifts. To make matters worse, some dumbass (not from my planet) calls in and compliments her on her spoiled little offspring. Barffff! Where is Linda Blair when I need her? Sadly, a large number of Grace fans (from this planet) take her sensational analysis seriously.

Bill Maher said it best "New rule: Nancy Grace has to prove she was somewhere else the day of the murder. *Any murder.* I'm not saying she did it, I'm just saying: I think most Americans are relieved to see Nancy Grace on TV, because it means she's not hiding in the backseat of your car with piano wire and those cold, black eyes."

Then there are the weather reporters. It's blowing a hurricane and they're standing on some tropical beach with their mouths malformed by the 70 mph wind. Their hair, along with roofs and plywood, is flying through the air. They put their lives and the cameraperson's life in danger. The producer, who you can't see on your screen, gives the signal to start the live transmission, and now in the middle of a Category 2 hurricane, years of meteorologist experience is broadcast to the world.

"It's possible that there could be some flight delays to the island today." Why did they say that? Just once, just one time, I'd like to see a big coconut fly though the air and WHACK – right across the weatherman's head, followed by my TV screen going blank. I'd like to see that just once.

Mike Tyson attempted to bite off Holyfield's ear and was disqualified. Then Mike said, "He has a cut on his ear, and he didn't want to fight." Why did he say that?

The captain of the crippled *Costa Concordia* cruise ship, Francesco Schettino, reportedly said the reason he was in a lifeboat while thousands of panic-stricken passengers and crew were trying to evacuate was because he "tripped" and fell into the rescue craft. Why did he say that?

When a few teenage girls at Fairbanks female prison in the Cayman Islands decided to write a complaint letter which mentioned the incompetence of some prison guards they were retaliated against 24 hours later. At 10 p.m. on December 4, 2010, a team of nine combat-booted Special Emergency Response Members were sent to the prison to remove an illicit cell phone from a teen girl who was calling her boyfriend. When Eric Bush, then Deputy First Officer for the Cayman Islands, was asked why nine Special ERT Officers (known as SWAT in the US) were needed to remove a cell phone from a 110-pound teen girl, he claimed, "The special officers were back-up." Why did he say that?

Seventy-four cell phones were confiscated at the men's prison the same year – yet no Special ERT team was deployed for these searches. So why did he say that? The president needs back-up in case of attempted assassination, uprising or riot, but to remove a cell phone from a teen girl? Well, I forgive Eric; after all he is an Earthling. Maybe your typical dimwitted Earthling may buy that story, but as for this Coherent, that bamboozlement isn't worth a flush down the toilet. In the same incident the guards decided to retaliate further for the letters so they conducted a "strip search" on the young teen girls without first checking the girl's property for the cell phone. When asked, why did they do that, the prison responds by saying, ***"Officers must first ensure that no inmate possesses any weapon and to reduce the risk of assault or harm when conducting any type of search."*** Wow, what a lie. Seventy-four cell phones were confiscated at the men's prison the same year... and no men were strip-searched. So, why did they say that? The Island's Complaints Commissioner summed it up: ***"In my opinion, the strip search was retaliatory and there is evidence to support this."*** Then she went on to say in a Prison Inspection Board meeting... ***"It was an outrageous act."*** Egg-in-the-face to the prison and Mr. Eric Bush. But why did they say that? On Planet Earth, when police investigate the police or when the prison officials investigate the prison officials you will get nothing more than a pile of bogus, misleading manure on paper. When prison guards strip-search teenage girls for a cell phone – yet the muscular, weight-lifting men inmates are not – it can only be summed up in one word: "cowardly." So why did they say that?

"Only two things are infinite, the universe and human stupidity, and I'm not sure about the former."
– Albert Einstein

I know why he said that
– Author

KIDS ON VACATION. BAD IDEA

Some parents are really stupid (yes, I know, I've said it before) especially new parents. OK, let's give the new parents some slack; we can forgive them for leaving the child in a minivan safety seat with the windows rolled up in the blazing sun while they pick up beer in the liquor store. We can understand that a new parent may forget to recap the bottle of sleeping pills left on the coffee table. We can pardon them if they have no fence around the swimming pool, but there is no forgiveness for taking the little darlings on a romantic Caribbean vacation. I see it all the time and their intentional obliteration of a vacation pisses me off.

Here come the new proud parents for their 10-day Caribbean vacation. They check in late with six pieces of luggage, diaper bags, bottles, a stroller, portable highchair, cases of sunscreen and their faces are already lobster-red from overstress. They drag the sleeping kid into the restaurant in a baby carrier, the band starts a loud calypso and now the infant starts to scream. The mother pulls out a boob and starts breastfeeding, the father is embarrassed so he goes outside to smoke a cigarette, the bartenders are gaping through the rum bottles to get a better look at mama's nice containers and their dinner of expensive lobster is getting cold. The weather for the next several days is perfect – just what they flew 3,000 miles for. The lagoon is enticing and the tropical sun is inviting them to the beach for a golden tan. Young spring-break bodies blanket the sand and the father wants to go out and play. He can't, however; he's babysitting because mom was up all night with a gripe-screaming toddler and she needs her sleep. He can't go outside because the infant may get sunburned and it would be hard to hit on those teen bunnies with a burping child on his shoulder. He wants a rum punch but mom would chew his ass out for drinking while babysitting. He turns on the TV and watches CNN. He could have done that in Chicago and saved $350 a day, plus airline tickets, plus the rent-a-car that hasn't moved from the hotel parking lot. It's 2 p.m., mother finally gets up, and she's in a foul mood because she also has the gripes (Montezuma's revenge). Dad has been ordered to find a drugstore somewhere on this island; mom needs gripe water and Pepto-Bismol.

"Great," he thinks, "I can get out of this room and explore a bit, drink some rum, smoke a Cuban cigar."

"Honey, take the baby with you, some fresh air may do her good. And don't drink while driving with the baby. You know you can't handle your rum... and don't smoke any cigars please."

"Yes, dear."

"Don't forget the diaper bag and sunscreen."

"Yes, dear."

"And take her little sun hat?"

"Yes, dear."

A few days later a babysitter is reserved through guest services. Mom and dad plan to go snorkeling and finally escape to some romantic cove for a picnic and love. The dread-locked Jamaican sitter shows up reeking of ganja.

"Ahhh, what a cute dalin' you 'ave 'er masta. Wha da child name?"

"You are the sitter?" mom and dad ask in unison.

"Ire, dat me."

The mom starts to read off the rules, the feeding times, nap times, medication needs... don't go outside, don't watch TV, don't... the sitter falls asleep mid-instructions. They cancel the sitter but she demands payment for an hour's work plus taxi fare back to the other side of the island. The father goes to file a complaint at the front desk and the snorkel boat captain is waiting for them.

"Sorry captain, we can't make it today, we have no babysitter."

"Hey, that's cool dude, but I'm keeping your deposit."

"Why? I told you we couldn't get a babysitter. It's the hotel's fault. They sent us some lazy, ganja-smokin' Jamaican who fell asleep before we even left the room. She was idle and useless."

The boat captain balls his fist. "Hey, dat' me mama you talkin' about."

Kapowww! Dad is on the floor. Mom walks into the lobby and sees dad on the floor. She gives him a good kick in the ass.... "I told you not to drink any rum!"

The baby screams and the staff can't control their laughter.

Healing the black eye he got from the black son of the Afro-Jamaican babysitter, he sits in his $350-per-night hotel room with the baby. Mom is frazzled, she needs a drink. At the beach bar she downs a few topical concoctions, she's getting sloshed. A big, muscular black man makes his move and buys her another round.

"So, you wan' go for a boat ride?" he offers.

"Oh that... that would be nice, but my husband he... oh, I'm pissed at him. He got bombed yesterday and passed out in the hotel lobby."

"Wha wrong wit 'im? A juicy, sweet mango like you? An' he leave you all alone?

"Yeah, screw him... let's go for a boat ride."

Later, as the Caribbean sun sets beyond the reef, the husband is pacing the floor. He hasn't seen mom since lunchtime.

"Hello... is this the front desk?"

"Yes sir, Mr. Jones. How's that black eye healing?"

"Never mind that. Has anyone seen my wife? She's gone missing."

"Oh, she's fine sir. She went with Captain Lanzo for a boat ride."

"A boat ride! Captain Lanzo! But it's 7 p.m. It's dark out there."

"Oh, don't worry sir, Captain Lanzo knows what he's doing. He takes all our guests on snorkeling trips."

"The same Captain Lanzo who... why he... who goes snorkeling at night?"

The irate dad snatches the little darling from her crib and makes his way towards the beach bar.

"Has anyone seen my wife?"

"She's with Captain Lanzo. There – I can see the lights of his boat beyond the reef," responds the bartender.

"Who goes snorkeling at night?" shouts a very distraught dad.

"You could be right," agrees the bartender. "But maybe they're fishing. Fishing is good after sunset."

Dad paces the beach, watching the boat lights in the distance. The baby is getting irritated now, even more so than dad. He hears a loud scream coming from the direction of the boat.

"Did you hear that? My wife's in danger! Call the Coast Guard!"

The hotel manager attempts to calm his guest with some words of reassurance. "Sir, she most likely hooked onto a big fish."

"Or a three-foot eel," snickers the bartender.

This wasn't looking good so a concerned lady offers to hold the baby while dad grabs a rental kayak and makes his way to the shore.

"Hey, what ya doin', mon! That's my kayak," says the beach attendant.

"I'll bring it right back. I need to rescue my wife. I just heard her screaming."

"Sir, you can rent it but I need you to fill out the insurance release and leave a deposit."

"Can't it wait till I get back? My wife's in danger. She's with Captain Lanzo, that asshole, and I'm going to kill him when I get my hands on him."

Now the young beach attendant is perturbed.

"Asshole? You're gonna kill him? That's my father you are going to kill!" KAPOWWW!

Dad is out in the sand and mom finally makes it to shore. She totally loses it when she sees her screaming baby in the arms of a stranger at the beach bar. She walks down to the beach and gives her unconsciousness husband a swift kick in the ass.

"Drunk again you useless idiot of a father... I'm on the first flight out of here tomorrow. Go rent another room. You are not sleeping with us tonight."

What's the moral of this story? Next time leave the kids at home. You should have used a condom.

"Learn from your parents' mistakes, use birth control!"

NEW AND IMPROVED

I love to go shopping in the huge supermarkets when visiting the U.S. The mountains of fresh vegetables, fruits and fried delights seem to add inches to my waistline before I ever reach the checkout counter. I always take note of the "new and improved items". Not that I am so gullible that I would fall for these advertising ploys. I am, however, amazed at how many Earthlings will pay extra money for things like a new and improved toothbrush. How do you improve a toothbrush? The drug section of the store is filled with an array of multicolored toothbrushes. Some have soft, hard and medium brushes. Some have a little rubber thingy on one end to get leftover pizza out of those hard-to-reach places. Others you can plug into the wall; they have little motors built inside so you don't have to move your hands up and down. Then there's the latest new-and-improved gimmick. I picked one off the shelf. Wow, this is a smart idea. It has a horizontal line painted on the brushes to help you take notice when the brushes are worn out. Is someone with a marketing degree actually provided an office and secretary to sit around and dream up new and improved attention-grabbers?

Yes, it must be so, because the grocery shelves are full of new and improved items... new and improved zip-lock bags, with a wider seal. A wider seal ? Yep, that's what it says: a wider seal. I'd rather have a bigger bag... who needs a wider seal? Or the new, large zip-lock bags with a handle so you can carry your wet bathing suit home from the beach. New and improved hydrogen peroxide... this one has a clear bottle instead of the brown bottle. Now you can see how much peroxide is left and pay 20 cents more for the convenience of having a clear bottle. However the directions say that hydrogen peroxide, H_2O_2, will turn into H_2O if exposed to sunlight, so best keep your new and improved peroxide in a cold, dark place underneath your bathroom sink – go figure!

Back to the toothbrush. It's not that the new and improved toothbrush is any better. It is simply that you believe that it is better and some will pay any price just to have it. It's clever marketing that has a plentiful supply of dim-wits to market to. So, yes the university graduate marketing specialist deserves an office and a secretary. If one chooses to be stupid – then let's not blame the marketing experts. If you believe the televangelist is going to release you from your wheelchair and send you to Heaven, then go ahead: give him 10 percent of your salary in tithing's – FOOL!

One company that makes paper towels has a "new and improved" stunt – they put fewer towels in the roll. A company executive explains: "We had to make the towel able to soak up more water and to cover the costs of this improvement, we slightly reduced the sheet count and size, and our consumers' response to these changes has been positive." Give me a break... I am sure they took a survey to see how many customers are happy with fewer towels and the survey proved in the company's favor. Give me a break Planet Earth. And what's up with the new and improved shampoo? I bought a bottle because the old and inferior shampoo was sold out. In my shower I still had a half-used bottle of the old version. While suds and water cascade from my hair I examine the old version. Same size bottle, same color shampoo, same manufacturer, so what's new and improved? I felt I had been swindled. Wrapped in a towel I was about to drive down to my local grocer and demand a refund when I noticed the "new and improved" component of the shampoo bottle. The latest version has small groves on the side of the bottle, so it will not slip from your hands while bathing. And there's more... it costs 22 cents more than the old version. Now that's clever, but it pisses me off. Back again to the "new and improved" toothbrush.

Even your average Earthling could not be conned by this marketing sham – no way! While I'm still examining the "new and improved" toothbrush an Earthling asks: "Hey is that the new and improved toothbrush?"

"Yes ma'am, it has a line on the brushes indicating when the brush is worn down and time to buy another. Isn't that clever... Here, would you like this one?" I say.

"No way, I don't want that, you can put it back."

What! Have my ears deceived me, have I actually run into a level-headed human?

Just as I was about to compliment her on her good judgment she says, "I want the blue colored one."

"You can fool all the people all of the time if the advertising is right and the budget is big enough."
– Joseph E. Levine

BRAZILIAN GIRL SELLS HER VIRGINITY

Now we're talking. This young lady is definitely from my planet. If you're gonna lose it anyway – why not sell it? Catarina Migliorini could gain $780,000 by giving up her virginity to a man from Japan known only as "Nastu." The sizzling hot 20-year-old Brazilian woman auctioned off her virginity online and now, by Brazilian standards, she could be a millionaire. Makes complete sense to me. This one-time event is not prostitution unless she continues to sell her goods after the big event. Catarina herself declares, "If you take a photograph and it is good, you are not considered a photographer." Right on, Catarina. You make sense on such a nonsensical planet.

The mysterious and obviously wealthy "Natsu" beat out five other bidders after an intense final day where the price of Catarina's asset jumped from $190,000 to the final $780,000 price tag. Now considering the lucky cherry picker is from Japan, Catarina may consider the following: It is alleged that Asian men have small penises. If that fable is true she may not lose her virginity at all yet be $780,000 richer. Should that be the case, I say go for it again Catarina. To hell with what the upright snobs of this planet think. The same act twice, if you still have your virginity left after the first act, would not make you an official prostitute, not on my planet anyway. And why does everyone give hookers such a hard time? Even phony clergymen love hookers.

On February 21, 1988 Pentecostal preacher and televangelist Jimmy Swaggart stood in front of his congregation, crying, whining and deplorably asking the Lord for forgiveness. He had been caught with a prostitute. "I have sinned, I have sinned," he admits as he stares up at the heavens. Then there's the aroused Catholic priests who regularly appear in the headlines after they're caught molesting an altar boy. These hypocritical bigots never cease to amaze me. Have they forgot what Jesus comments in Matthew 5:27-28: "But I say to you that everyone who looks at a woman lustfully has already committed adultery with her in his heart." Jimmy should have prayed that they legalize prostitution. Prostitutes, whores, ladies of the night... why not legalize them? Prostitutes need to make a living and old men, preachers and horny teenage boys need to get laid. On Planet Coherent, prostitutes are appreciated and held in high esteem. After all, what's the harm? It's totally wrong when some hooker gets arrested for having consensual sex with some shy teenage boy who spends all his time masturbating. Prostitution is legal in most of Europe including England, France, Wales, Denmark, and also in most of Mexico, Brazil, Israel, Australia and many other countries. It is either legal or very accepted in most of the Philippines. And in the most unlikely place like Iran, they have so-called

"temporary wives" also known as "sighih" .Wake up
America! Wake up Caribbean islands! If it feels good
– legalize it. As long as we keep prostitution illegal,
pimps are profiting and old men are denied what is
rightfully theirs – fornication. In 1994, the then
Attorney General Dr. Jocelyn Elders, was invited to
speak at a United Nations forum. She was asked
whether it would be appropriate to promote
masturbation as a means of preventing young
people from engaging in riskier forms of sexual
activity. She replied, "I think that it is part of human
sexuality, and perhaps it should be taught." Well
that makes sense to me, but guess what happened?
She was fired by President Bill Clinton. Yes, the
same Bill Clinton, 42nd president of the United
States, who allegedly received White House oral sex
from Monica Lewinsky. Or was it the other way
around? Whatever. He was impeached by the House
of Representatives on two charges, one of perjury
and one of obstruction of justice, and then later was
acquitted by the Senate. America – what a country!
The president fires the attorney general for
promoting masturbation and then the president gets
fired for promoting blow jobs and then he is re-
hired because he's the president. Only in America –
what a country, please grant me citizenship.

Models sell their bodies, actors sell their bodies,
yet when a hooker sells her body – she is arrested.
That pisses me off. Then there's the health issue
such as sexually-transmitted diseases like
Gonorrhea. That stuff can kill you. Well, so can
alcohol and tobacco. You need a license to sell
alcohol and tobacco. Your bar or liquor store is

regularly inspected by the State Alcohol Beverage and Tobacco Control Board, so why not sell licenses to prostitutes and give them regular VD inspections? Arrest figures for prostitution vary, but some data has it as more than 100,000 annually in the U.S. So let's sell hookers a license for $100 per year. That would equal about $10 million. The money could be used for education and to help cut inflation – and it would make a lot of old men happy. Nobody ever listens to me.

"Prostitutes are way better than marriage. Why buy a whole cow, when you only want a glass of milk."
– I didn't say that... Author unknown

AND NOW THE GRAND FINALE

Just when you think you have heard it all, all of the stupidity of this planet... here comes a black hurricane. Yes, it appears some racist politician has found yet something else to be unreasonable about. Black congresswoman Sheila Jackson Lee of Houston reportedly complained that the names of hurricanes are all Caucasian sounding names.

OK, we have the Black Movie Awards, Black Miss Teen Awards, Black Music Awards, Soul Train Awards and Black Miss Nude. I have no grudge against these ceremonies... but black hurricanes? She was obviously not thinking when she filed that complaint, which of course is a normal practice for most politicians. Ms Jackson demands that some of these deadly, destructive storms should reflect African-American culture (or something like that?). She would also like the weather reports to be broadcast in 'language' that street people can understand because one of the problems that happened in New Orleans during Katrina was that black people couldn't understand the seriousness of the situation due to the racially biased language of the weather report. Racially biased language? Now this remark earns a top spot in the OBTUSE awards.

Since when are words like run, evacuate, get help, seek shelter and get the f **k out of here considered racially biased verbal communication?

Sheila Jackson Lee could be the most dim-witted person in or out of Congress. If there were such a thing as the OBTUSE award for dense, she would take home the grand prize. Hey, I'm not making this up. I guess what she means is that it is too hard for an African-American person to understand when the weatherman says the winds are going to blow at 140mph and you need to seek shelter. She is an insult to her race. I couldn't believe that a congressperson, who collects her salary from taxpayers of all races, said such an ignorant thing. Why did she say that? Did she really say that? I looked it up on the Internet and, sure enough, she said that. If I were a black man, this woman would get a good whack from me and some of my colorful friends. My initial thought was, "You can't fix stupid." But I wanted to give her the benefit of the doubt, so I did some investigating of my own.

"What do you think about it?" I ask my close friend Andy. (Andy is more bronze than black). "I don't give a damn what they call a hurricane as long as it doesn't come my way."

"What's your opinion Larry?" (Larry is a few shades darker than Andy). A hurricane is a hurricane. I don't need to look that word up in any dictionary... it means run for cover. Name it Obama or George Bush, they're all the same – dangerous!"

"What's your opinion Chester?" (Chester is very black). "Dat Shelia woman, she mad. In Kingston we been licked wit plenty hurricane – all wit white man name. Only a white mon can cause so much destruction, so why name a storm Jafaris or Ebony?"

Good point Chester!

There is some gender discrimination on my planet – all hurricanes have female names. Hurricanes are like women: when they come, they're wet and wild, but when they leave they take your house and car.

Probably running a close race with Shelia is Rep. Todd Akin, former congressman for Missouri. He said openly that he is opposed to abortion, even in a case of rape. He said that victims of "legitimate rape" have unnamed biological defenses that prevent pregnancy. "If it's a legitimate rape, the female body has ways to try to shut that whole thing down." OMG... both Shelia and Todd need total expulsion from sanity.

"Suppose you were an idiot, and suppose you were a member of Congress; but I repeat myself."
– Mark Twain

An actual law made by lawmakers: *"If you plan to jump off a building in New York, you could be arrested and they could give you a death penalty!"*

STOP THE PRESS

Sorry Sheila Jackson Lee, sorry Todd Atkin, move over. It has just come to my attention that someone else deserves the OBTUSE award – so give it back. In a CITES meeting held in Harare, Zimbabwe (CITES is the Convention on International Trade in Endangered Species of Wild Fauna and Flora, whose aim is to ensure that international trade in specimens of wild animals and plants does not threaten their survival) President Robert Mugabe declared that he will *not* put a ban on ivory because elephants took up a lot of space and drank too much water. Elephants would have to pay for their room and board with their ivory. His comment makes Shelia Jackson's hurricane grievance look like an international peace treaty. The majority of nations (including many in Africa) have always considered Mugabe mentally disordered. The Uganda-born Archbishop of York labeled Mugabe as "the worst kind of racist dictator." Mugabe undoubtedly agreed with the African bishop by calling himself the "The Hitler of the time." OK, President Mugabe, please come to the stage to accept your OBTUSE award and, please, we want don't want an acceptance speech.

SUMMING IT ALL UP

I hate to say it. I hate to be so cliché, so unoriginal, but here goes: "Common sense is not common anymore." Yes, it's an overused axiom, but it's a common sense saying that makes common sense. The necessary level of understanding and decision-making that gets us by day-to-day is simply not widespread on this planet called Earth. NFL players shoot themselves in the ass and child molesters are sent back into society to molest again. Yes, I am on the wrong planet and I'm sure I'll be reminded of that more frequently after publishing this book. Am I right all of the time? Of course not. According to your average Earthling I'm hardly ever right, I do however find comfort to know that so many great, wise and famous people agree with me (RE: Go back to the first ten pages and re-read the section titled – I'M NOT THE ONLY ONE).

On my planet I'm always right. On Planet Coherent I am always in control. In fact, there, I am the master, ruler and dictator of my world. I am the most powerful, popular person on my planet. I know what you're thinking right about now: What a cheeky creature he is, not to mention arrogant and conceited. Well, there's good reason for my smugness. After typing thousands of words for this manuscript, I've come to the conclusion that I am the only person on my imaginary planet called Coherent.

Following a recent blood and urine test, a CT scan and eye examination I asked my doctor, "Well, what do you think? Am I on the wrong planet?"

"Well, he said, you think too much and drink too much. From a professional medical point of view you're rather normal. Having said that, it is possible you have a neurological disorder on the autistic spectrum. Then again, he continued, I'm not certain because one of the things wrong with the world today is that there's too much certainty in things that people really shouldn't be certain about, such as metaphysical concepts and religion."

His diagnosis made no sense at all. Why didn't he just say I was nothing more than an eccentric oddball, as I've been told so often by others? Now, he may think that but he would never say that. After all, I'm the customer and he's a businessman, so it's best for him to beat around the bush and confuse me with medical terms rather than get to the point. One person described me as the most intellectual person on my imaginary planet with a population of one. Who gave me such a compliment? Me, of course.

And just when I think I may have been a bit unreasonable in my criticism of your average Earthling... just when I want to give more Earthlings the benefit of the doubt... just when I was about to apologize for some of my crude rudeness in this publication... I read the newspaper and there is a story about a Rhode Island school superintendent who ended the district's father-daughter dances and mother-son ballgames to comply with a state gender discrimination law, prompting some to complain that the move is an example of political correctness gone awry. What? Political correctness gone awry? No, no, no... such political correctness is downright idiotic. Why mince words? Maybe I'm the one who needs a good whack across the head.

COULD THERE BE SUCH A PLACE AS COHERENT?

Well from my non-astronomer, layman's point of view I say, "Why not?" Why should Planet Earth be the only sphere entitled to have mountains, rivers, oceans and idiots? It just doesn't seem fair does it? Astronomers have calculated that six percent of the galaxy's 75 billion or so red dwarfs (stars smaller and dimmer than the Earth's own sun) probably host habitable, roughly Earth-size planets. That works out to at least 4.5 billion such "alien Earths", the closest of which might be found a mere dozen light-years away, researchers say. This information bears strongly on the search for Earth-like alien planets, since roughly 75 percent of the galaxy's 100 billion or so stars are red dwarfs. What's a red dwarf anyway? An Indian midget maybe? No, I'll let Wikipedia explain:

"A red dwarf is a small and relatively cool star on the main sequence, either late K or M spectral type. Red dwarfs range in mass from a low of 0.075 solar masses (the upper limit for a brown

dwarf) to about 50 percent of the Sun and have a surface temperature of less than 4,000 K. Red dwarfs are by far the most common type of star in the Milky Way galaxy, at least in the neighborhood of the Sun, but due to their low luminosity, individual red dwarfs cannot easily be observed. From Earth, not one is visible to the naked eye. Proxima Centauri, the nearest star to the Sun, is a red dwarf (Type M5, apparent magnitude 11.05), as are twenty of the next thirty nearest. According to some estimates, red dwarfs make up three-quarters of the stars in our galaxy."

Well there you have it. After reading all that astronomical mumbo-jumbo I need a drink. However the point is made (though there is no real evidence) there's bound to be a Coherent somewhere amongst the possible 4.5 billion "alien Earths". Be it so, there could be planets that hold nothing but tropical islands, planets with nothing but water, planets with nothing but rivers of rum and fields of fine tobacco to roll fine Cuban cigars. And planets of more idiots or planets of Coherents. Considering that even the wisest astronomers are not 100 percent sure of the galaxies make up, my theory could be spot on. There could be a planet where common sense is abundant and idiocy is rare. A planet where politicians are honest and lawyers are forthright. A planet where pedophiles are castrated and the likes of Jimmy Swaggart and Benny Hinn are flogged in the town square. Flogged by the poor fools who donated to their organizations so these crafty evangelist can purchase Lear jets, Rolexes and prostitutes. The fact that people still follow these insane, phony, religious freaks just shows how many people in this Planet Earth are hopeless.

Having said all that, be it nonsense or wisdom, I do believe in reincarnation. When you're dead and gone I doubt seriously that you will end up playing the harp on a cloud or sinking in a river of fire and brimstone. What makes more sense is that you will either be eaten by worms or caught up in someone's nostrils as your ashes spread across the countryside. Re-embodiment however could be as possible as deja vu. Why not? Haven't you ever had a discussion with some moron and thought to yourself, "Gee, I've heard this stupid notion before." If whoever is in control of reincarnation chooses that I spend another lifetime on Earth, then please, please, please punish me by transforming me into a pig living on Big Majors Cay in the Bahamas, I deserve it. That way I will not be a nuisance to anyone, I'll help keep down pollution by eating garbage and I'll not write a follow-up to this questionable publication.

No Man is an Island. Says who? John Donne. He was making reference to the human condition, we as humans need interaction with other humans, not pigs. Trying to live alone, without association with other people is debilitating and self-defeating. Whether we like others is not the point; we cannot do without them, so says John. Well that theory may have worked in the year 1572 when John Donne was born in England, but if he lived nowadays with 7.118 billion Earthlings he may rewrite his famous phrase with this idiom: "Every man needs an island." Well,

I do anyway in order to escape the overpopulation of idiots. In 1572 there was no TV, Internet or air travel. You did not get up every morning and read a newspaper or watch the international news where the absurdity of the planet was exposed. So hiding away on an island in 1572 was just not as alluring as it is nowadays.

In the meantime... "Beam me up Scotty."

END

"Never argue with a fool -- people might not be able to tell the difference."

ABOUT THE AUTHOR

H. G. Nowak (The Barefoot Man) is the creator of several other books including *Which Way to the Islands, The Cruisin Boozin Song Book, The People Time Forgot, and The ABC Book of the Cayman Islands.* Known best for his double innuendo tropical songs on some 22 albums, his original tunes are a mix of Calypso, Country and Reggae garnished with a 90% dose of humor. He lives in the village of Breakers on the island of Grand Cayman and still performs for tourists several nights per week (when he's not off on some remote island fishing). He is also a contributing writer for several island publications.

The Barefoot Man's music may be ordered directly from his website at Barefootman.com.

Made in the USA
Lexington, KY
24 June 2018